KINANE

'A heart-warming story of a family who worked their way up from humble beginnings to worldwide fame, this book is a thoroughly enjoyable read.'
Irish Racing Post

'If you are a fan of horse racing then look no further than *Kinane*.'
Belfast Telegraph

'A cracking read.'
Irish Field

'A remarkable story.'
Irish Daily Star Sunday

ANNE HOLLAND has written numerous non-fiction books related to horses and horse-racing, including *The Grand National* and *In The Blood*, both published by The O'Brien Press. She was also a successful amateur rider.

KINANE

A REMARKABLE RACING FAMILY

Anne Holland

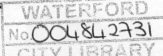

THE O'BRIEN PRESS
DUBLIN

First published 2010
by The O'Brien Press Ltd
12 Terenure Road East, Rathgar, Dublin 6, Ireland
Tel: +353 1 4923333; Fax: +353 1 4922777; Email: books@obrien.ie
Website: www.obrien.ie
This edition first published 2011

ISBN: 978-1-84717-291-4

British Library Cataloguing-in-publication Data
A catalogue record for this title is available from the British Library

2 3 4 5 6 7 8 9 10
11 12 13 14 15

Layout and design by The Little Red Pen
Printed and bound by CPI Group (UK) Ltd, Croydon, CR0 4YY
The paper used in this book is produced using pulp from managed forests.

Picture credits: *Front cover*: Top: Brown's Barn ridden by Jayo Kinane in the Power's Gold Cup. Bottom:
The Kinane Family (both photographs Healy Racing). *Back cover*: Sea the Stars & Mick Kinane winning
the Tattersall's Millions, 2009 (photograph by Healy Racing). *Picture section 1*: Anne Holland: p. 1 top;
Healy Racing: p. 3 top, p. 6 bottom, p. 7 bottom; Bobby Hopkins, Glasnevin: p. 4; *Evening Herald*: p. 5;
Sunday Press: p. 6 top; Ruth Rogers, Ashbourne, County Meath: p. 8 bottom. *Picture section 2*: Healy
Racing: p. 1 top, p. 2 top, p. 3 top and bottom, p. 4 bottom, p. 6 top, p. 7 top and bottom; Colin Turner:
p. 1 bottom; Ruth Rogers, Ashbourne, County Meath: p. 2 bottom; Anne Holland: p. 5 bottom, p. 6
bottom; Noel Mullins: p. 6 centre, p. 8 top and bottom.

Every effort has been made to trace holders of copyright material used in this book, but if infringement
of copyright has inadvertently occurred, the publishers ask the copyright holders to contact them immediately.
The publisher would like to thank Tommy, Susan, Antoinette, Brendan and Paul Kinane for all their help
in sourcing photographs for this book.

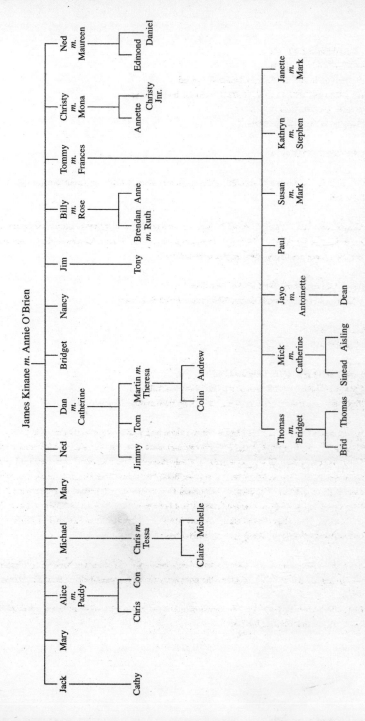

A selected Kinane family tree, showing those members mentioned in this account.

Contents

Foreword by Tommy Kinane   ix

Acknowledgements   xi

Prologue   xiii

1   The Kinanes of Cashel: Tommy   1

2   Tommy's brothers and sisters   23

3   'We want to be jump jockeys!'   43

4   The coalman's horse and others   59

5   Cheltenham calls: Monksfield   66

6   A splinter off the old block: Thomas   86

7   Off to a flying start: Mick   98

8   A love of horses: Jayo   110

9   The one that got away? Paul   132

10   Tommy's racing nephews   138

11   'As rare as hens' teeth': the Kinanes at Ballydoyle   168

12   Mick seeing stars   174

Epilogue: Tommy travels the world   188

Foreword

My main aim for this book was to have it written before all of my generation had passed on, and I am indebted to my daughter, Susan, whose idea it was, and who undertook the initial research and sifted through many photograph albums. It was while I was talking with the author, Anne Holland, in Punchestown, after the launch of her book *In The Blood,* that she agreed to take it on professionally.

I was one of fourteen children, and only three of us are left: my sister Nancy, who is eighty-two, my youngest brother Ned and myself. My parents were James, known as Jim, Kinane and Annie (née O'Brien) who was herself one of sixteen children. Of their eight surviving sons, seven rode in races: Mick, Dan, Jim, Billy, Christy, Ned and myself.

I am proud of the racing successes of all four of my sons equally: Thomas, Michael, Jayo and Paul. I also have numerous nephews who rode, many with considerable success. All of them are included in this book. I had seven uncles who emigrated to

America (as well as my eldest brother); two came back, and one of those was killed out hunting on the Limerick, Tipperary and Cork borders.

In addition to the some nineteen Kinanes and one Keane (a son of my sister, Alice Keane) who all rode racing, I have discovered that we are related to Daniel (Danny) Maher. He was champion jockey in America in 1898 and twice UK champion jockey where he rode 1,421 winners and won nine Classics, including the Derby three times. So you could say racing was in our blood.

Tommy Kinane
August 2010

Acknowledgements

With grateful thanks to all who have given their time and help for this book, especially to so many members of the remarkable Kinane family in telling their stories, lending photographs and checking and re-checking facts; also to the incomparable Martin Murphy at Horse Racing Ireland; Derek Gay and Mick Mutlow, Aintree experts; Tony Reilly; Aidan O'Brien; Timmie Hyde; Jane Clarke, Curator of the Aintree Museum and to The O'Brien Press and Liz Hudson.

The passing of time can play tricks with memory and although I have tried to verify dates, times, places, horse's names and so on, if some mistakes have slipped through, I apologise.

Prologue

Tommy Kinane fixed the photograph of his second son, Mick, riding his final winner, into his last large album; it was on Nebula Storm in a two-year-old maiden at Leopardstown on 5 November 2009, and appropriately Mick was wearing the yellow and blue colours made famous by Sea The Stars. Tommy placed the album neatly onto the shelf, padded over the pile carpet, and sank into the deep blue and white upholstered armchair, resting his slippered feet onto the plush footstool. Carrie jumped up onto his lap, and as he stroked the Patterdale terrier's sleek black coat he allowed himself a contented smile. Job done.

The albums had been meticulously maintained by his wife Frances for more than forty years, documenting the many Kinane feats and successes on and off the racetrack for more than five decades; it was the one thing Tommy had continued for her after her unexpected death just a year and a half before their Golden Wedding anniversary. It had been quite a journey.

1

The Kinanes of Cashel

Tommy (b. 3 October 1933)

Heading out of Cashel on the Dundrum Road, the mighty Rock of Cashel standing sentinel over the surrounding fertile countryside, the traveller passes Brittas House Stud on the left and the old Cashel racecourse on the right, where today the defunct grandstand looks a forlorn concrete monolith, incongruous amid the cattle grazing around it. Round another bend, and there on the left is Camas Park Stud, home to the Hyde family. Its green pastures lead down to the banks of the river Suir, crossed by an ancient stone bridge. A couple of hundred yards further on, beyond the Drehideenglashanatooha Bridge at Ballinahinch, a right turn leads into a narrow lane, pretty in the early morning sunlight. On the left, a quarter of a mile down, are the ivy-clad remains of a small cottage that, eighty years ago, was bursting at the seams.

Tommy was the seventh son of the fourteen children of James (Jim) and Annie Kinane. Jim was the son of a well-to-do grocer and hardware monger in Tipperary town. Apart from helping in the family business Jim was also a stonemason, working for the council, and he built part of the wall around the Rock of Cashel. After his marriage, his family disowned him, believing Annie 'wasn't good enough'. Tommy's interest in horses came from Annie while another enduring family interest, ballroom dancing, came from Jim and, more specifically, Jim's brother Mick, who was Champion Irish dancer and taught in Dublin.

On this particular morning, Annie finished the hand milking of the three cows and three goats and went indoors to get the children ready for school. Jim had already left for work. In the evening he would join the older children in hoeing their acre of land, wresting every possible ounce of food for the family from its soil.

Their eldest son, Jack, had already left home and had emigrated to America. Ned and Mick had gone to England, and their first daughter, Mary, had died at the age of seven. Inside the cottage, the older children Alice and the second Mary helped get the middle ones – Dan, Bridget and Nancy – ready. The younger twins, Jim and Billy, tucked in to their porridge, and Tommy, not yet school age, raced over to greet his mother as she checked that Christy was asleep in the tea chest. She turned to comb Tommy's shock of golden curls with one hand and patted her swollen belly with the other. She hoped this latest pregnancy would be her last.

She waved the rest off to school, the older ones marshalling the younger for the half-mile walk. Later in the day she might sit by the turf fire, poking it into action, but not yet. For now, Annie was 'free' to tend to the baby and toddler, the house and the cooking, the pigs and turkeys and to pour the precious milk into the churn. She took care to add a little of the goats' milk to that of the cows' – no wonder her cows' milk regularly tested the best for cream. She harnessed the donkey, hauled the two heavy churns into the cart lent by neighbour Paddy Taylor, settled the children and set off for the creamery 3 miles away in Ardmayle.

They were hard times, which made Annie a tough character. Her life was not without tragedy as not only Mary had died but her son Ned was also soon to die. He worked in a rubber factory in London and died in his early twenties from a lung disease. Later that year, in November 1937, Annie gave birth to her last child, another son, and he was also named Ned.

The youngest quintet, all boys, shared much of their childhood. One of their pastimes was ferreting, and from the time he could barely walk Tommy went out by lamplight with the twins, Jim and Billy, and, when they were old enough, Christy and Ned. The rewards were good: £1 per rabbit, and that was in the mid-1940s.

The school in Ballinahinch had one teacher, Josie Roache. In order to remain open the school had to have eleven pupils per teacher; therefore, to help keep up the numbers, Annie Kinane despatched her youngest children there as early as possible. Christy joined Nancy, Jim, Billy and Tommy at a tender age. One day, Billy had transgressed in some way and was told to put out his right hand for the cane. Billy had a nasty sore on this hand and proffered his left instead.

Miss Roache insisted on slapping him on the sore hand. At this, young Tommy saw red. Even from a young age the Kinane children were not afraid to fight to defend a sibling – of course they sometimes fought each other too. Enraged like a bull, Tommy charged up to the teacher and kicked her on the shin. Mayhem ensued: she called the parish priest, Father Mackey, and Tommy was made to go down on his knees and apologise.

Now, Annie Kinane was strict with her children – she had to be with such a large number – but when she heard what had happened she was not going to take it. Next morning, she prepared the donkey and cart, put all five school-age children in and drove them to teacher Jim Ryan in Ardmayle. He enrolled them all, and they spent the rest of their school years there, usually walking or running the 3 miles to Ardmayle, sometimes barefooted in the summer.

Billy was by now mad keen on hunting and would spend every minute he could following the hounds. One day, when the hunt was nearby, he, Jim and Tommy mitched off from school to follow. Soon they were whooping excitedly, but they hadn't reckoned on their mother being on her way to the creamery at the same time, to collect skimmed milk for the pigs. She recognised Billy's excited voice, and later, when she pointedly asked him how school was, he realised they had been rumbled . . .

Another time, Tommy was irked by a girl at the school who told on him for some long-since-forgotten misdemeanour, resulting in the teacher slapping both his hands ten times with a leather strap. Furious, he waited for the girl after school at the bridge over the wide and fast-flowing river Suir, grabbed her and hung her over the edge of the parapet. It was only when his

Kinane: A Remarkable Racing Family

friends saw what was happening that they intervened and pulled her to safety. Tommy made good friends at school and remains in touch with a number of those who are still alive.

With the farm donkey in constant use between the shafts and the pony commandeered by the older children, it was to neighbouring farmer, Paddy Taylor, that Tommy gravitated, running across about three fields instead of going the longer way round by road. There he began riding the grey pony and two horses bareback, which doubtless accounted for his trademark balance and 'stickability' on a horse.

It was also Paddy and Maggie Taylor who initially taught him and some of his sisters to dance. Waltzing around the kitchen to music from a wind-up gramophone, Tommy found himself instinctively drawn to the beautiful art.

By the time he was twelve or thirteen, Tommy spent his weekends and school holidays on Paddy's farm, hand milking, tilling beet, turnips and mangels and piking hay, and he used to drive the pony with the milk churns to Ardmayle. He also became one of the best men to hoe and could skilfully 'thin out to one' – what's more, he still does, using that same original hoe.

One spring day, when Tommy was fourteen, he was guiding a pair of Paddy's horses, tilling the vegetables, when he heard that the local Tipperary Foxhounds point-to-point was taking place in Tullamaine. He wanted to go. Paddy Taylor wanted him to finish his task. Tommy handed the reins over to his mentor and announced that he was going. He sped down to his mother, who lent him her high-nelly bike and gave him five shillings, then off he pedalled the 15 miles to the venue.

He hid the bike in a hedge, hopped over a ditch and walked across the field towards the tents and horses and spectators. Before he got there he noticed a bunch of men in a circle around another man who was holding some cards. Man after man lost money but Tommy kept watching. He was hungry, and he intended to make himself some extra money. Once he was certain of how the three-card trick was working he put in the whole five shillings. He lost it.

The next morning, Annie dropped her fourteen-year-old son down to Tim Hyde at Camas Park, barely half a mile away, to begin serving his time as an apprentice. His wage was £1 per week – not ungenerous compared with some other stables.

It was an environment Tommy revelled in. Already used to hard work, neat turn-out and strict discipline, he was now surrounded by horses, both thoroughbreds and showjumpers, and other lads, such as Tighe Ryan, Johnny Kenneally, Jimmy Bourke, Mickey Browne and, in due course, his younger brother Christy. In no time he was riding work (galloping) and schooling racehorses, and, during summer evenings, he would also be schooling showjumpers, including one called Hack On, owned by the McDowells, the Dublin jewellers.

One Christmas Eve, Tommy and Tighe had been in to town, and it was late when they returned to the dormitory above the stables. The other lads were already asleep, but two of them had cider bottles beside their beds; one was three-quarters full and the other half. Deciding to help themselves to an early Christmas present, it was Tommy who drank the most. He didn't like the taste, but he was determined not to leave any. In the morning, red-faced as the others laughed at him, he discovered the joke had backfired. The bottles had been filled with the other lads' pee.

Whether because of that or because of a frugal streak, Tommy, who never much liked alcohol anyway, became a Pioneer at the age of fifteen, a pledge he remained true to until his late sixties or early seventies when he began to imbibe the occasional glass of brandy while out dancing. He also reckons that by neither drinking nor smoking throughout his working life he was able to afford a new car each year.

His riding ability progressed in leaps and bounds at Camas Park, and he continued to learn the importance of discipline, punctuality and cleanliness. 'Tim Hyde was a great man to work for and totally honest. When he was coming into the yard he would whistle loudly so that if anyone was slacking they had time to look sharp.'

As a teenager, Tommy also learnt how to box. He used to go round to a neighbour, Willie Doherty, where, as a younger child, he and his siblings had often sought refuge from their mother when times were tough. His tutor in Willie Doherty's kitchen was the local police constable, later Sergeant Ryan, and, before long, Tommy would take on any lad willing to fight him.

In later years, when in London, he boxed for the Lyons Club in Cadby Hall, an office and factory complex in Hammersmith. He became well respected on the open-air boxing circuit in Battersea Park and Clapham Common. He taught all his children bar the youngest, Janette, to box – it was a skill that came in handy for both Susan and Kathryn in fending off unwelcome suitors.

When he was in his twenties and working for his brother, Dan, Tommy boxed for Callan Boxing Club. In what was to prove his last fight he knocked out the reigning Leinster light-weight champion, but he was disqualified for an allegedly low blow. Later, he discovered that the referee was his opponent's coach. 'A while after, the opponent told me he knew the blow wasn't low,' Tommy says, 'and I never put on a glove again after that.'

His three older sons, Thomas, Mick and Jayo, were all boxing champions of Tipperary, Waterford and Munster many times, for weights ranging from 6 to 9 stone.

Showjumping in the summer was nearly as important as racing the rest of the year in Tim Hyde's at Camas Park, and there were some summer evenings when Tommy would be standing bareback on a horse while jumping stone walls – balance again. He rode in some showjumping events locally and in Cork riding a 14.2-hand mare called Croguemore, but he didn't find the sport fast enough for his liking, and so it was left to his brother Christy to taste frequent success with the mare at shows all over Munster.

It was July 1951, and Tommy, along with his brother Christy and box-driver Charlie Byrne, escorted four horses down to the Clonakilty show in west Cork, staying overnight. Under his care were Heartbreaker, owned by Mrs Peg Watt, Hack On, Cahirdaniel and one other. When Tommy gave his boss Tim Hyde a leg-up onto Heartbreaker the next day, it was just a simple, everyday routine. The class was a novice competition and so the fences were not unduly fearsome. Tommy watched with mild interest from the ringside as the round progressed and the pair approached the double bank, with a dyke on both sides. Something made the horse stop at the last minute, and Tim, in the forward position for jumping, was thrown over the horse's head into the back of the dyke. Unfortunately, the horse followed, landing on top of him.

Tommy ran.

The first-aid personnel reached the stricken rider and began trying to pull him out from underneath the horse.

'Don't touch me,' Tim at once instructed, 'my back is broken.'

The horse was wearing studs in its shoes (used in that sport, and sometimes on the road, to give extra grip, especially round sharp corners; racehorses do not wear them). Two of the studs had pierced Tim's spine.

It was a sombre journey back to Camas Park. 'We drove through Cahir and New Inn, heading for Cashel, knowing he was seriously hurt, but it was to be a few weeks before we knew just how bad it was,' Tommy remembers. Tim's wife Jenny, sister of trainer Willie O'Grady, was at home with her young family, Mary, Timmy, Sheila, Geraldine and Carmel. The news of the accident had been broken to her by telephone. Tim Hyde, who had won the 1939 Grand National at Aintree on Workman and the 1946 Cheltenham Gold Cup on Prince Regent, and who was one of the most highly respected riders and trainers in Ireland, had broken his back in a low-key novice showjumping competition. He would never walk again.

It wasn't possible for Jenny to continue with the training, although, with the help of head lad Jimmy Bourke, she gave it a valiant try. She had five children aged from eleven years down to four and now a desperately sick husband. Some of the owners took their horses away. There was nothing for it but to shut up shop; not only would the horses be dispersed but the lads would also have to go. Tommy briefly worked for Chaloner 'Chally' Chute in Doneen, Patrickswell, County Limerick, for £1, 5 s. a week but he was soon to accept the guidance of Tim Hyde's head lad, Jimmy Bourke.

Jimmy found jobs for most of the Hyde lads in the UK, and the first boss that Tommy headed over to was Tom Pettifer, of the Pettifers Green Oils family, who manufactured a remedy for various equine and farm-animal ailments. In the early 1900s the oils had been produced from a tarred wooden shed with a corrugated iron roof known as the Spice House in the pretty village of Eydon, Northamptonshire, where the Pettifers had lived since 1687; in 1960 the company was awarded a royal warrant. Tom Pettifer was now based near Didcot in Oxfordshire.

It was a restless time for Tommy at first. He had never lived far from home, and he had never before been to England. The train pulled into Didcot Station where Tommy and Tighe were greeted by the secretary, Miss Carter, who was driving a soft-topped green Riley sportscar that sped them to the Pettifers' stable yard at Letcombe Bassett. Tommy lodged with a Mrs Kelly in Letcombe Regis for ten months but began to feel more at home when he moved on to join Tom Yates and had digs on a farm with Mr and Mrs Percy Tapper – 'She was a lady.' The stable jockeys at Tom Yates's were Brendan O'Neill and then Michael Grassick. An outside jockey used on occasion was Dick Francis.

The experience was not without its lighter moments, as when newly arrived in the area from Catholic Ireland Tommy was out one evening with some of the local lads. They were strolling through a park when Tommy spotted what he thought was a balloon. He stooped to retrieve it, intending to blow it up, but the other, more worldly-wise lads stopped him just in time – Tommy had never seen a condom before.

It was while at Tom Yates's that the name 'T. Kinane' first went up on a number board. It was for a two-year-old race at Bath, an attractive course high on the escarpment above the historic and beautiful Roman-influenced city. Tommy was seventeen, but, far from having an apprentices' race for his first ride, he was thrown in against the likes of Australian ace Scobie Breasley, Willie Snaith, Tommy Gosling, Ken Gethin and Bill Rickaby.

Tommy was riding a filly with the word Princess in her name, and Scobie was riding a stable companion. As Tommy cantered down to the start he found the unfamiliar 2-pound saddle so uncomfortable that he nearly fell off. He hadn't enjoyed having to waste down to 8 stone 11 pounds either. It was a tape start, and Tommy remained in mid-division for most of the race, which was won by a lad even younger than him – a sixteen-year-old jockey by the name of Lester Piggott.

Lester became a legend of the racing world and beyond, but at the time the jockey held in the highest esteem was Gordon Richards, who became the only jockey ever to be knighted. Tommy remembers that on the day of his first race ride, word came back that Gordon Richards had ridden four winners at Kempton – a fine feat. In 1932 (the year before Tommy was born), Richards rode a staggering total of 259 winners in one season, a record that, with more and faster transport at his disposal, was only bettered in 2002 by jump jockey A. P. (Tony) McCoy. Sir Gordon's career number of 4,870 wins in Britain remains a record.

At the time, it was customary for a winning rider to give the lad leading up the horse £1. Tommy looked after a top 2-mile chaser called Limb of the Law. One day, the gelding was pitched against the reigning Champion Chaser Rose Park. Dick Francis and Limb of the Law duly beat the champion that day, but no pound was forthcoming – not until twenty-one years later, that is, when Tommy was at Aintree donning his silks to ride Pearl of Montreal in the Grand National. Dick Francis was also there, signing books. Tommy approached him and introduced himself. 'Do you know you owe me a pound?'

'How so?' Dick asked.

On hearing the reason, Dick put his hand in his pocket, pulled out a £1 note, wrote a signed message that the debt was now honoured and handed it over. Today the note is among the racing memorabilia in Tommy's home.

While Tommy was still working for Tom Yates, he was approached by Tim Adamthwaite, a private trainer in the neighbouring village of Letcombe Regis, to ask if he would try riding a horse that none of his staff could handle.

Traditionally, after an early morning start, stable lads have a few hours off in the afternoon before returning for evening stables, which involves 'setting fair', that is, picking up the droppings in the stable, having fully mucked it out in the morning. It is often also the time when a trainer inspects each horse, and the lad must have his horses gleaming for this, with hooves picked out and tails brushed as well. After that, they are fed, and the lads are then free, though the head lad or the trainer may return later for a last feed and to check that all is well.

The system meant that Tommy was free to help Tim Adamthwaite in the afternoons. The horse in question, Arabian Chase, was a full horse (not gelded). When Tommy got on, the horse, as usual, reared. 'Put a pair of blinkers on him and bring me a length of polythene pipe,' Tommy requested. Importantly, the horse never succeeded in throwing Tommy off. Gradually, Tommy sorted him out, rode work on him and schooled him over obstacles.

Tommy's reward was to be given the ride racing on him, and their first appearance was at Wincanton in Somerset when, Tommy recalls, Fred Winter rode the winner. Next it was on to Towcester in Northamptonshire, another big, galloping course, and Arabian Chase 'ran a cracker', finishing third. Bob Turnell was aboard the winner.

Tommy was twenty-one years old – his career could have burgeoned from here. Instead, by his own choice, he quit. 'I got a bee in my bonnet about going to Australia,' he says. He handed in his notice to Tom Yates. 'You're a fool,' Tom told him, 'you have the makings of a champion jockey.' But Tommy was adamant. The racing world might never have heard of Tommy Kinane again.

His older sisters Mary and Alice were in London and often visited Tommy. They told him stories of their youngest sister, Nancy, in Australia. Tommy was young, and the glamour and riches of Down Under appealed, and he decided to emigrate. But he got no further than London.

He lodged in Cadby Hall (before it became an iconic Lyons Corner House). First he spent ten months working on the line of the Lyons factory in Hammersmith. Then he went to the job offices, where he met a guy from Galway who was working for McAlpine. The firm was constructing a huge hangar-like building nearly half a mile long for testing submarines near Heathrow. He asked Tommy if he would like a job.

In 1955, the factory foreman gave him a pick and shovel

and told him to dig some foundations for a wall. 'There were no diggers in those days,' Tommy says, 'just us Irish navvies.' Tommy may have been small in stature but he soon proved his strength and tenacity, and, after his time at McAlpine, he became a scaffolder's mate. Within six months Tommy had become a fully qualified scaffolder himself, working for Higgs & Hill in Baker Street.

Tommy did keep his hand in with horses by riding out for Tim Adamthwaite at weekends.

Although he was from the depths of the Tipperary countryside, there was nevertheless something that Tommy liked about London. Part of this was the attractive girls and part of it was dancing – rekindling his interest that had begun with a wind-up gramophone in Paddy Taylor's Tipperary kitchen. Two or three nights a week would see him at the dance halls where he could hold his own with the best of dancers in the top-of-the-range Hammersmith Palais. He escorted a beauty queen, and another girl he courted for about three months was called Diana Cummins from Abbeyleix, County Laois; she was a stunning but fiery blonde. He was dancing with her one night at the Emerald when one of Tommy's workmates, Jim O'Brien from Knockavilla, between Cashel and Dundrum, arrived. With him was his sister, Frances. *She's not bad-looking,* Tommy thought to himself. Then he saw her dancing; she was like a ballerina. Boldly, he asked her if he could see her home. She turned him down.

A few weeks later, when still partnering Diana, he met

Frances again. This time, Frances agreed to his request. Diana was left to find her own way home, but came to the couple's wedding, as did the beauty queen. 'I can honestly say, I never looked at another woman again after I met Frances,' Tommy says. 'She was a lady and a perfect mother, perfect housewife and great to be with wherever we went. She always greeted me with a smile on her face. She was a brilliant cook. She would conjure up a needle and thread if needed no matter where we were. And she was my best friend in life. We might have had one row in forty-eight and a half years, but you couldn't really argue with her – she would open her two big blue eyes and say, "Go to God."'

Frances was one of sixteen O'Briens. Their eldest son Thomas says, 'None of the sixteen in her family had anything to do with racing. She was quiet, but if she spoke up we knew about it. Father would be dominant, but she could get him to do anything she wanted. He's a flamboyant character and a very determined person, but she had the key.'

The couple were married in Fulham in December 1956. Frances's sisters were present, as were Tommy's siblings, Billy, Mary and Alice. Tommy was earning good money as a scaffolder: £33 per week, a large sum in those days, but that was for seven days a week and so there was to be no honeymoon. 'But we went dancing a few nights a week.' To be dancing with his bride was sufficient for Tommy.

Their first child, Thomas, was born on 8 July 1957.

A few months later, out of the blue, Tommy's brother,

Dan, who was training in Mullinahone, County Tipperary, asked Tommy if he would work for him. The wages would be £2 per week. Tommy had had his carefree young manhood in London; he was now married with a baby son. The temptation to return to his homeland was stronger than he had imagined.

Dan urged him to come. Tommy did not need much persuading but first he talked it over with Frances. It was not going to be easy for her because she would have to live with Tommy's parents while he was away working during the week – difficult at the best of times, let alone with a young family.

Frances was good-natured and wise. She advised Tommy that if that was what he wanted then he should give it a go. She was also prepared to cope with living with her in-laws. In October 1957, Frances's brother Jim and his wife Mary waved Tommy, Frances and baby Thomas off from Euston Station. 'Frances was a saint,' Tommy recalls, 'and got on with my mother who would not have been the easiest.'

For Tommy, the new job meant a regular Monday morning cycle of 22 miles from Ballinahinch, through Cashel town and out beyond Fethard to Mullinahone where Dan trained. If the stable was quiet he could get home at the weekend, but it wasn't guaranteed.

One of the first horses that Tommy rode for Dan was Kilmore. He rode the future Aintree Grand National winner in his first four or five races. When the horse finally did win, it was Tommy's younger brother Christy who was on board at the now-defunct Mullingar racecourse.

In those impoverished days, the moment a horse looked like being good, it was almost inevitable that it would be sold to England, where there were many more wealthy owners than in Ireland. So, Kilmore was sold to England, and, trained by Ryan Price, Fred Winter rode him to victory over perpetual bridesmaid Wyndburgh in 'the big one' of 1962.

Tommy and Thomas, and others like them, sometimes rode for trainers at half fee. Why? Because if they didn't accept the deal the trainer would put up someone else, and naturally the Kinanes wanted to ride. In Tommy's case, a half fee would be £2.50. That could not happen today as all finances are administered by Horse Racing Ireland.

On 8 January 1958, three months after leaving London and making his return to racing, Tommy Kinane had his first ride in Leopardstown. Smart, spacious, set in the Dublin suburbs and home today to the Champion Stakes on the flat and the Lexus Chase at the Christmas National Hunt festival, Leopardstown could be called Ireland's premier course. Tommy's mount was Trade Union, trained by Dan, in a handicap hurdle, and it brought him his first win at the age of twenty-five. He beat Papus, ridden by Paddy Powell Junior and trained by Harry de Bromhead (grandfather of trainer Henry de Bromhead). At the time, the riding fee for a jump jockey was £7 and £10 for a winner; the flat riding fee was £5. (Two of Tommy's four sons also rode their first winners at Leopardstown: Mick on his debut on Muscari in March 1975 and Paul riding Champagne Brigade, also as a teenager in 1984.)

Tommy was showing promise as a professional jockey, but work was hard, and the journey between Dan's stables and his parents and family was long, so he was naturally eager to have a home of his own for his wife and family. Frances was patiently coping with young Thomas and, in June 1959, with the newly born Michael (Mick). Tommy managed to find a house near Callan, County Kilkenny, with an acre on which they could milk one cow and till the rest, to provide enough vegetables to feed the family. At last he had a home of his own, and, with his riding career going well, it seemed not unreasonable to ask his brother Dan for a £1 wage rise, to bring his weekly packet to £3. Dan refused, and Tommy walked out and left him.

What to do now? He had a new house, a growing family and no job. He soon found work with one Andy Kennedy, for whom he won a nice race on Foolish Heart, and he had been there for about a year when, out of the blue, he received a call from Arthur Morris asking him to come to Powerstown Park (Clonmel) as private trainer (officially head lad) and jockey. It was a big leg-up for Tommy Kinane. He sold his house, and the family moved into the large house and stables provided for him at the top of the hill beside the racecourse: Clonmel town lay in the valley below, which was bisected by the river Suir, and the Comeragh Mountains rose in the distance. It was an ideal venue for training, and Tommy did well. His family was also increasing – James (Jayo) and Susan were born while the family was there.

There were good days and bad. One time Tommy thumbed a lift to Mallow racecourse in County Cork, his intended runner having travelled earlier. Once there, he picked up an additional two spare rides, and won on both of them. By contrast, in the spring of 1961, in Clonmel, Tommy suffered what should have been a career-ending fall which nearly threatened his life.

He had three runners as trainer, and he was to ride them. He was in chipper mood, confident that all three – Fall of France, Prince Gainmore and Mutton Cutlet in the bumper – might win. The first runner, Fall of France, looked ready to set the ball rolling as he headed to the last fence in the lead. Tommy was never afraid of riding hard into the last fence especially if he was being pressed, as he was now by a horse called Grooms-man, ridden by Bobby Beasley. Fall of France turned a som-ersault, and Tommy was catapulted headlong into the ground. He lay inert, and he was seen to on the ground by a doctor. He struggled to his feet and insisted he was OK to ride in the next race. Cantering to the start on Prince Gainmore he began feeling weak and light-headed. He took one hand off the rein and slapped his cheek hard with the flat of his hand. No doubt adrenalin and competitive spirit did the rest: he won the race, beating his brother Christy on Vulcania and Jim Cash on Ban-ree. He managed to weigh in and then, relinquishing his last ride, somehow staggered home and to bed.

In the morning, he couldn't lift his head off the pillow. Using his hands, he grabbed hold of his thick, fair hair and pulled himself up. As he walked into the kitchen, Arthur Mor-ris's sister, Peggy, who was staying, remarked, 'You don't look well.' She rang 'Sawbones' Magnier (uncle of John Magnier of

Coolmore). When he arrived, he took one look at Tommy and had him taken to Cashel Hospital immediately. Tommy had fractured a vertebra at the back of his neck – he can insert a finger into the hole today – and so began several weeks of lying flat on his back surrounded by sandbags. At length he was able to go home and begin the rehabilitation. He couldn't walk, let alone ride. His young sons, Thomas and Mick, taught him how to walk again, and before long he was able to ride one of their ponies. Eleven weeks after the accident, he was back race riding.

In 1962, when Tommy had been in Powerstown Park for two or three years, he was approached by Michael Purcell, a member of a prominent family in the area. Michael had a yard at Farney Castle, Holy Cross, and he asked Tommy to come as private trainer, which still went down in the official books as 'head lad', the owner holding the licence to train. Part of the job was that he could continue race riding. There were now four children in Tommy's family – Thomas, Mick, Jayo and Susan – and the proposition was another rung up the ladder for him, so he didn't take too much persuasion. Kathyrn and Paul were born while the family lived in Holy Cross.

Farney Castle is an extended and adapted fifteenth-century battlemented castle which was added to in Gothic Revival style in the eighteenth century. It is set within mature gardens and contains fine outbuildings and a demesne bridge. It has been a part of the area since medieval times – its neighbour Holy Cross Abbey is even older. Moving there was the start of a great period for Tommy, which coincided with the blossoming of his riding career. He was in constant demand as a tough, competent lightweight – the winners were beginning to pile in too.

Tommy was making money and, in truth, was riding so much that training was playing second fiddle. He relinquished his arrangement with Michael Purcell, left Farney Castle and bought a 90-acre farm at Crohane, set on a steep hill near the town of Killenaule, which became the family home for the next twenty years. Killenaule lies on the river Bauteogue, just south of the Slieveardagh Hills, with many ancient ring forts and castles in the area. Although well inland, Killenaule was the target of Scandinavian invasions in the ninth century. There was even a battle at Crohane in 852, but the only battles there from 1969 were on the racecourse.

2

Tommy's brothers and sisters

Jack (1911–1996)

Tommy never met his eldest brother, Jack. Born on 19 February 1911, Jack had emigrated to America before Tommy was born. Not only did horses never enter Jack's life but also for much of it he remained unaware that on the other side of the pond he had a family that was becoming increasingly respected and renowned in racing.

Jack's youngest daughter Cathy believed she was part of a very small family apart from her brother and three sisters. She grew up with almost no other relatives – or so she thought. Her mother was orphaned at the age of five, and her father Jack had never been back to Ireland since the day he left. One day, when Cathy was in her early twenties, she happened to find an old envelope with the words 'Kinane' and 'Cashel' on it. She wrote to the Post Office in Cashel, and the end result of that was that she travelled over, met and stayed with her grandparents Jim and Annie Kinane, and their son Billy and his wife Rose, in Ballinahinch.

That was in the early 1960s, and staying with her 'new' grandparents was a bit of an eye-opener after life in Connecticut. For starters, Cathy didn't feel very welcome, and then she wanted to let the dogs and cats into the house as she would at home – 'but that didn't go down well.' On another occasion, Annie gave her a spoon and asked her to go and get some potatoes. 'So off I set looking for a grocer!' Cathy says. 'It was Annie who set the work ethic for the boys, but she was difficult, and very tough on the girls. My grandfather Jim was a darling man.'

It was to be another twenty-five years before Cathy plucked up courage to return to Ireland, 'and this time they all seemed happy to see me.' She brought two suitcases full of presents and party treats with her for the various children and stayed with Tommy, who was by then living in Holy Cross. With the exception of Tommy's wife Frances, Cathy banned all adults from the party and produced American toys, cakes and sodas from the suitcases for the children. One of the goodies she produced was a fruit flan, and Thomas recalls how his father Tommy jokingly ran off with it. 'If she hadn't chased him he would not have bothered with it; as it was, they chased him until he was found in a ditch eating it.'

Then there was a dinner 'with all my uncles' – Tommy and his various brothers. Having grown up with no relatives, Cathy was suddenly surrounded by them. 'I just sat and looked at them,' Cathy says, welling up with tears as she remembers. Of her uncle, Tommy, she says, 'It would take twelve people to keep up with him.' She talks about her cousin, Mick, 'my little baby who devoted his life to a craft that came from his father. Uncle Tom was a great jockey but then along came the little star who never said anything.' Cathy, talking from her home in Connecticut, adds that her own son, Andrew, is like that, a 'very quiet personality'. 'I am very proud of Mick, but the price of stardom is a hard thing – you have to give up a lot. When you are as big as he is, people try and hang on to your coat-tails.'

Cathy worked for the UN in hospitality for thirty years among young Irish people who would love to have gone home but couldn't afford to. Now, having reconnected with her own family, she says simply, 'It is wonderful to see success stories – though I don't know one end of a horse from the other!'

Jack was a mechanic, and horses never came into his life, although he enjoyed fishing and shooting. Cathy took home lots of photographs from her visits to Ireland, spread them out on a table in front of Jack and quietly left, not knowing whether or not he ever looked at them. Jack died in 1996, aged well into his eighties.

Mary, Alice, Michael, Mary and Ned

Annie and Jim's Mary was the second-born, but she died at the age of seven. Alice, Michael and a second Mary followed, and all were to move permanently to England. Mary married

Frank Maher of Bansha who became a well-known flat race jockey in Newmarket, and Alice married Paddy Keane. Paddy rode many point-to-point winners, and both his sons, Chris and Con, rode. Chris served his time with Major Snead at Wantage and used to pony race at Hawthorn Hill, and Con rode out on his father's horses in his early teens when Paddy was training at Northolt, near the airport. Although he didn't race himself, Con has always followed his family's exploits, especially those of his uncle Tommy and cousin Mick. A retired barber from Slough, he enjoys racing at Windsor, Newmarket, Kempton and Sandown Park, while he will be 'glued' to the television for Cheltenham each March. Con used to go there when Tommy was riding and will never forget his victory in the Champion Hurdle, the coach trip there and the celebration meal in the Orchard Hotel, Ruislip, after.

Michael had a somewhat chequered life, marrying four times, but he inherited typical Kinane horsemanship. He moved to England at a young age and married his first wife, an Irish girl, when she was eighteen. Sadly she died in childbirth along with the unborn baby. He then married Valerie, who produced two sons, Jim and Mick, and his third marriage was to an English girl, Gill White, who produced two more sons for him: Chris, who became a capable professional jockey, and Alec. There was one more wife to come, Nancy, and she gave him two daughters: Alice and Jenny. Chris was the only one who pursued a career with horses.

Michael rode in a number of point-to-points in the Home

Counties around London, winning a few, but it was hunting he loved with a passion. He was also a good showjumper and was successful at the top venues such as the Horse of the Year Show, then held in White City, and at Hickstead, Douglas Bunn's famous Sussex venue. Really serious injuries in showjumping are comparatively rare, but Michael had a fall at Hickstead that resulted in him badly injuring one of his legs.

In later years, Tommy got Michael back for their mother's funeral in January 1971, and he remained in Ireland for many years, eventually being reunited with his son, Chris. He became travelling head lad for Edward O'Grady and retired to Mullinahone, where he was once again enfolded within the Kinane clan. In later years, Mick moved to Wales, where he settled down with Nancy and his daughters, Jenny and Alice. He mainly bred dogs and trained greyhounds until he separated from Nancy. His health deteriorated quite soon after that, and he died in 1994.

Ned was the sixth child born to Jim and Annie Kinane, and he too – times being what they were – moved to London, where he worked in a rubber factory, developed lung disease and died in his early twenties. Tommy can just remember him when he visited home.

Dan, Bridget and Nancy

Dan began his career working for Major Gibson, of the Tipperary Farmers Hunt, which suited him, given his love of hunting, but by the time his first son, Jimmy, was born he was working for trainer Jack Lombard in Kanturk, County Cork. He also worked for Vincent O'Brien when Vincent was still in Churchtown, County Cork, before he moved to Ballydoyle.

From there, Dan moved to Longfield House at Goolds Cross near Cashel – 'I think the Coolmore crowd have it now,' says Jimmy – and, after training there, he bought the home that his children first really remember: Kilvenmon, near Mullinahone. It was an old rectory four storeys high, with twenty-two rooms, lying between Kilkenny and Clonmel – not far from Fethard. He bought it for about £1,000. Dan married Catherine, and they had three sons – Jimmy, Tom and Martin, all of whom rode winners – and three daughters. Sadly, at only forty-three years of age, Catherine died. The children ranged from twenty-one years down to nine, and it was a tough time for them. Tragically, Tom was also to die at a young age.

Dan both rode and trained a number of good winners, and some amazing future stars passed through his hands. He not only trained Kilmore but he was also responsible for breaking in Flyingbolt and Rondetto when he was in Mullinahone. Both became steeplechasers of the highest calibre, and Rondetto, trained by Bob Turnell, ran in the Aintree Grand National five times. He fell twice when leading, including at the infamous twenty-third (Foinavon) fence and eventually finished a gallant third to Highland Wedding in 1969 at the age of fourteen.

Flyingbolt, trained by Tom Dreaper, is remembered as the horse who might have been as good as Arkle, but, as they were in the same stable, they never raced against each other. Like his illustrious stable companion, Flyingbolt also conceded huge lumps of weight when winning some of National Hunt racing's greatest handicaps, including the Irish National at Fairyhouse and the Massey Ferguson at Cheltenham. At the National Hunt Festival at which Arkle won his third successive Cheltenham Gold Cup in 1966, Flyingbolt won the 2-mile Champion Chase and, one day later, finished third in the Champion Hurdle.

As for Kilmore, Dan rode him twenty-two times, Christy rode him in nine races and Tommy in seven, and all three brothers won races on him, most notably the Munster National at Limerick for Christy in 1960. He was sold for £3,000 in February 1961 and joined trainer Ryan Price in Sussex. He finished fifth in that year's Grand National, and, at the veteran age of twelve, in heavy ground in 1962, he won the great race, ridden by Fred Winter.

When Dan was training, with considerable success, his younger brothers Tommy and Christy not only both rode for him but also had spells of working for him.

Dan Kinane rode a number of horses for Vincent O'Brien, usually early in their career. Some of these were Lucky Dome, Alberoni, Castledermot and Galation, who twice went on to finish runner-up in the Champion Hurdle. In Buttevant, near Churchtown, before Vincent moved to Ballydoyle, Dan rode work on the likes of Cottage Rake and Hatton's Grace, two of Vincent's big stars before he turned to training for the flat. Cottage Rake won three Cheltenham Gold Cups from 1948 to

1950, and Hatton's Grace not only won the Champion Hurdle three times successively between 1949 and 1951 but also had the speed to win the Irish Cesarewitch twice as well as an Irish Lincolnshire.

Two more daughters were born to Annie Kinane after Dan: Bridget, who left Ireland for the UK at eighteen and eventually made her home in Australia, and Nancy, who lives in Nottingham.

Jim (1931–2003) and Billy (1931–2009)

Twins Jim and Billy were born in Old Kinanes' near Cashel on 10 July 1931 and spent the first five years of their lives there before the family moved a few hundred yards up to Ballinahinch, where Billy's widow Rose lives now.

Jim started off working for Vincent O'Brien and then succumbed to the lure of London for a spell. Nevertheless, he was to return to Ireland. His first race-riding win was in a novice chase in Tramore that, remarkably, his twin Billy had won the year before. But, like his younger brother Ned, Jim was to spend much of his working life in hunting stables in Limerick. He had eight children, and two of his three sons are very tall, but Tony rode as an amateur.

It was almost inevitable that Billy would follow his family members into racing, although from an early age he also loved hunting. He scarpered from school in order to follow the hounds, and in later years he hunted a pack of beagles on a Sunday. The little hounds sought their quarry, the hare, across the fields and coverts surrounding Ballinahinch, west of Cashel.

Legend has it that the gap in the distant Galtee Mountains was the result of the Devil biting a lump out after St Patrick banished him from one of the mountain caves. The Devil dumped it on the place that is now Cashel, the reputed site of the conversion of the King of Munster by St Patrick in the fifth century. The hounds would hunt the banks of the river Suir or around Cashel racecourse, and often they ran in the shadow of the mighty Rock of Cashel.

Billy's first job at sixteen was with the O'Ryans at Ballahurst, County Tipperary, and, after a few years there, he moved to another part of historic Ireland – this one much more relevant to racing. He signed on with Chally Chute on the Curragh. After about three years, Billy joined his younger brother Tommy on the building sites of London, staying with him at Cadby Hall, Hammersmith. Billy married Rose Walsh from Brownstown, on the Curragh, when he was in London.

About two years later, Billy moved back to the Curragh, but with increasing weight this time it was to Dan Moore's yard he went. There, one of the horses he looked after was L'Escargot – although Billy had moved on to Mick O'Toole by the time that exceptional horse had won two Cheltenham Gold Cups and an Aintree Grand National.

Billy rode in a number of races, and his first win was for the Kennedy family in an opportunity chase in Tramore, riding a horse called Loyal Star. A year later, his twin Jim, a beautiful horseman, rode his first winner in the very same race for Henry Harty.

In about 1970, Billy, Rose and their children, Brendan and Anne, moved back to the bungalow at Ballinahinch. Billy began working for Vincent O'Brien and remained at Ballydoyle for the rest of his working life, breaking and backing the yearlings and riding the two-year-olds from Lyonstown, about a mile from Ballydoyle. One of the perks of the job was flying to the USA each autumn, with the head man and senior groom, to bring home the yearlings that Vincent had bought in the world-renowned Keeneland Sales in Kentucky.

The list of horses that Billy was first to ride reads like a Who's Who of the thoroughbred world: Epsom Derby winners Nijinsky, Roberto, The Minstrel and Golden Fleece; dual Prix de l'Arc de Triomphe winner Alleged; Law Society; Fairy King; Sadler's Wells; Be My Guest; and Storm Bird.

It was from Storm Bird that Billy got the worst fall of his career. He was inside the stable, where he was backing the horse for the first time. Twice the colt jumped into the feed manger, and eventually he got rid of his rider. 'I don't think he broke anything,' Billy's son Brendan recalls, 'he just got hurt.' Storm Bird, for his part, went on to win the Dewhurst Stakes as a two-year-old. Billy had some favourite sayings in life, chief of which was, 'The two most dangerous things in life are a woman's mouth and a horse's hind legs.'

Around about the time of the cloning of Dolly the sheep in 1996, Billy Kinane theorised that if a jockey were to be cloned then it would be his nephew Mick Kinane – for his size, stature, attitude, presence and strength – in short, he was the epitome of what a jockey should be. His son, Brendan, says, 'As a family, we would ask, "Were we biased?" Answer, yes – but it's true. We may never see Mick's like again; his qualities were similar to those of Sea The Stars, and providence brought them together.'

Billy Kinane died in 2009. Mick was (and doubtless still is) a regular visitor to his widow Rose, whenever he happens to be in the area. Brendan says, 'Mick would sit on the couch drinking tea, eating cake, so unassuming that you'd never know he was a jockey, let alone a famous one.'

Christy (1934–2007)

Born fifteen months after Tommy, Christy Kinane was a competent rider and an even better trainer who was universally popular. He was known as a jovial character who could talk to a tinker or a king. He could be very funny, always joking and leg-pulling with anyone between the age of nine and ninety. He was also a superb dancer, as his widow Mona testifies.

Christy shared many of his childhood and schoolboy memories with Tommy. At the age of fifteen he worked for Vincent O'Brien for four and a half years before moving on to Timmy Hyde. He rode his first winner from there, Might of the West, and had about nine wins all told for Timmy Hyde, before moving on to Mickey Browne nearby at Mockler's Hill in the mid-1950s. In 1959, Christy, like Tommy before him, moved to his older brother, Dan, for four or five years and rode for another ten years, with considerable success.

Christy went to scale at 9 stone 7 pounds when he dead-heated for the prestigious Galway Hurdle in 1961 on New-grove, trained by Vincent Leevey, with Cygne Noir, ridden by Pat Taaffe. He bagged even bigger chasing prizes, including the 1960 Powers Gold Cup at Fairyhouse on Owen Sedge – the seven-year-old was owned and trained by F. D. Farmer just out-side Naas. Like Tommy, he also won a Kerry National, in 1964 on Packed Home, trained by Dan Kinane and owned by Mrs J. J. Burns, carrying 9 stone 7 pounds. The gelding only went up 3 pounds in the weights the following year when Dan put up Charlie Finnegan to win the race in successive years.

There was one year when Christy was one of three jockeys vying for the Irish National Hunt Jockeys Championship. On his last ride of the season he was leading at the last fence in Limer-ick but his horse fell, and he was beaten for the title by one win.

The year of 1965 proved memorable for Christy Kinane. He married Mona Maher in October, and, although they 'had £10 between them', he bought the house and yard at the Green, Cashel. It was to become his home for the rest of his life, and Mona still lives there, although the fields that they used to look out upon across the road are now mostly covered in houses.

In the period between the purchase and his marriage, he had one of those rare racing accidents that didn't involve a fall. He was riding a horse in Limerick called Maxwell House when he collided with a rival in mid-air. The stirrup iron of the rider next to him banged into him so hard that his leg was broken. Bent over

Above: Tommy Kinane pictured at home in County Kildare in 2010, with his dog, Carrie.
Below: Tommy Kinane as a young jockey in the 1950s in Berkshire, England.

Above: Tommy and Frances on their wedding day in Fulham, London, in December 1956.
Below: Ned (left) and Christy (right) Kinane in their family home, at Ballinahinch with their mother Annie behind (left).

Above: Tim Hyde (owner), his daughter Carol Swan (jockey), Christy Kinane Snr (trainer), Isthatafact (horse), Michael Scanlon (lad), and Mrs Trish Hyde.
Below: Billy Kinane with Sadler's Wells.

Leopardstown 1958: Tommy Kinane on his first winner, Trade Union, trained by his brother Dan (to the right, wearing cap) and led in by owner's wife Mrs Rita Purcell.

Fifteen-year-old Mick (left) and Tommy Kinane appeared in the *Evening Herald* on 20 March 1975: 'Three days after winning the 6st 7lb title in the Munster Juvenile boxing championships young Michael made his racecourse debut at Leopardstown ... He romped home on the 16/1 shot Muscari ... Looks like we'll be meeting Michael again.'

Above: Thomas, Jayo and Tommy: 'A family with a winning streak', *Sunday Press*, 6 April 1975.
Below: Jayo in action winning in Roscommon on Jaytek Boy, owned by Jim and Eleanor Cringan, and trained by Tommy Kinane.

Above: Thomas, Edmond, Ned, Paul, Tommy and Kathryn.
Below: Paul Kinane riding his first winner, Champagne Brigade, on his first ride in Leopardstown, beating Hearns Hotel ridden by Tommy Carmody. The horse was trained by Tommy for owner David Giles.

Above: Tommy Kinane in the colours of the horse for which he is best remembered, Monksfield.

Below: Injury prevented Tommy riding Monksfield to victory in Liverpool in 1978, shortly after their joint Champion Hurdle success. He is seen here, sporting a plaid tam o'shanter, greeting Monksfield in the winner's enclosure.

double in pain, the other jockeys had to help him pull up at the end of the race.

As a trainer from about 1965 (while still race riding), Christy earned a reputation for being a successful winning trainer and for starting off future jockeys such as Michael Byrne, Enda Bolger (who brought a mare, Gemelek, with him), Phil Ryan (who rode a lot of winners) and Michael Molony. Some of the young lads would arrive barely knowing how to tack up a horse but, almost inevitably, after Christy had got them going well enough to win a few bumpers – the Irish National Hunt flat races that provide a 'nursery school' for novice riders as well as young horses – they would move on to bigger yards. In the locality this would often be to Vincent or his son David O'Brien where they could probably find greater opportunities and earn more money.

Christy hung up his own racing boots in 1969, the year his son Christy was born. His daughter Annette had been born in 1966. One of Christy's last riding winners was in a chase on Western Problem in Fairyhouse in 1969.

Christy was clever at placing horses. While the smart stables went off to Cheltenham, he would lay one or two out for the Aintree meeting, which was less of a festival in those days. He won a hurdle race there in two successive years with Cooch Behar, owned by Dom O'Brien. The first year, as a four-year-old, Cooch Behar was still a maiden, having only had one previous race when second in a maiden hurdle at Leopardstown. For the Liverpool race, Mwanadike was favourite but Cooch

Behar made all in the hands of Liam O'Donnell to beat him. Mwanadike turned the tables on him in Punchestown where he trailed in last, but he ended the season by landing odds of 3–1 on in a Limerick hurdle.

The next season was a busy one in which Cooch Behar took on the best of the generation as well as future stars and some past ones – horses such as Monksfield, Skymas, Hilly Way, Prominent King, Tied Cottage, Chinrullah, Beacon Light, Night Nurse and Peterhof. His Liverpool win this time was a lucky one, for Beacon Light had it well sewn up at the last when he fell. Cooch Behar and Liam O'Donnell turned out again the next day to take part in the epic Night Nurse–Monksfield dead heat. Cooch Behar was not disgraced. The following month he won a hurdle in Down Royal ridden by Ted Walsh.

Among Dom O'Brien's other good horses which Christy trained was Raleighstown, successful for both Thomas Kinane and Ted Walsh. Dom O'Brien and Dom McParland were probably Christy's most prominent owners over the years, and he won many races for them. Mona remembers Dom McParland as a big gambler and a great loser: 'if one lost he would just shake his shoulders and walk on.' Dom O'Brien, lucky with his horses, suffered a fatal heart attack at a very young age.

Christy's canniness at placing is illustrated by the time when he entered a horse called Isthatafact in Limerick Junction (now Tipperary) on the same day as the Aintree Grand National. It meant the local betting shop was many times busier than usual with housewives putting their small bets on the National, and so the money piling in for the Kinane-trained horse went unnoticed and the odds were not cut. Mona believes owner Peter Gormley won about £60,000 that day – and rewarded Christy well for his coup.

Among other long-standing and reliable owners were Jack McGinley (for whom Christy trained Owenius to win the 1978 Munster National), Paddy Purcell, John O'Connor, Paul Ryan and John O'Leary. Many were farming clientele, and training fees were sometimes paid for in hay and straw. Owenius himself was swapped in a deal for a calf from horse dealer Mick English. When he arrived, the 'wee horse' proved to be just that: he was barely 15 hands high. He grew, and he was tough too. As an eight-year-old he ran fourteen times, placing second or third seven times. The season before that he ran a healthy ten times, when he won a maiden hurdle early on and a novice chase near the end of the season.

Paul Ryan also bred some of his successful horses, among them Pauline's Fancy and Arctic Mist, trained by Christy. Christy trained mainly National Hunt horses though he had a few runners on the flat. He held the distinction of having trained winners on every course in Ireland with the exception of the Curragh. He did train one exceptional sprinter called Flower from Heaven for Dingle owner Billy Granville, and she won six sprints, including in the Phoenix Park.

Christy also trained a winner at Laytown, a grey filly called Reneagh. The only authorised beach racing, Laytown is held once a year and has an atmosphere all of its own.

Perhaps the most famous horse to pass through Christy's hands was Bregawn, who so memorably went on to lead home Michael Dickinson's famous five in the 1983 Cheltenham Gold Cup. Bregawn was bred by J. Fitzgerald, and Christy bought him off Joe Crowley, Aidan O'Brien's father-in-law and himself a talented trainer – as was his daughter Frances, married to flat jockey Pat Smullen.

In 1991, Christy Kinane suffered a heart attack, followed a year later by a successful bypass operation. He died in November 2007, but, as Mona says, 'The operation gave him sixteen extra years.'

Ned (b. 1937)

Ned is Tommy's youngest and only surviving brother. He lives today beside the yard at Crohane from which Tommy trained for twenty years and where Ned acted as head man and all-round helper. At times his duties even included childminding. Ned's life was intertwined with Tommy's at several stages but ultimately it was hunting rather than racing that became his greatest equestrian love.

The youngest of the sons, he grew up in Ballinahinch surrounded by ponies, and hunting was a natural part of childhood. Showjumping also became one of his passions. He left school at sixteen and worked for Miss Piery Edwards whose stud near Golden was to breed the 1981 English 2,000 Guineas winner To-Agori-Mou. From there he went to the Curragh as a lad for Paddy

(Darkie) Prendergast in the mid-1950s where the best horse he looked after was Hindu Festival, owned by the Myerscough family. The colt finished third in the Irish 2,000 Guineas, second to Ballymoss in the Irish Derby and won the 1957 Ormonde Stakes in Chester.

Ned moved on to Martin Quirke, also on the Curragh, but after a few months the lure of London – and a bigger wage – beckoned. Tommy was already there, and Ned joined him, working for three years in Cadby Hall on the Lyons factory conveyer belt. But, as with Tommy, the love of horses and Ireland beckoned again. Ned went back to train privately for Mrs Willington at Shinrone, County Offaly, before joining Tommy in Powerstown Park, Clonmel.

Ned's race riding was limited, but there was one occasion when he rode in a novice chase in Tramore, where he finished down the field. In the same race, his brother, Christy, fell off a horse called Clovis owned by another brother, Jim, and trained by Mickey Browne.

But the shifting sands were still at play. Ned moved to Lord Harrington in Limerick for a year, followed by another spell in London and then Somerset, where he trained for J. H. Toby Cobden at Martock and rode in a hurdle race. He also became involved in showjumping again through Tom Brake. One day he received a letter from Lord Harrington asking him to return. Ned was now married to Maureen; he was ready to settle down. The letter marked the start of a remarkable phase in his life where he was preparing up to nine hunters for a meet and was hunting himself up to five days a week, with the Limerick Hunt, the Scarteen (Black and Tans), the Galway Blazers, the Tipperary and, in Cork, the Duhallow. It also sealed a friendship with Lord Harrington that lasted until the peer died more than forty years later. Throughout that period there was never a summer that the pair didn't go fishing together from an island on Lough Derg.

Ned and Maureen were to have two sons, Edmond and Daniel. Maureen passed away in January 2010.

Ned Kinane enjoyed some memorable days hunting with the Limerick, bringing on young horses for Lord Harrington. There was one time when he and Lady Hilton Green, a 'goer' who saw no danger, got away alone with hounds – a rare and special, spine-tingling experience. On one occasion, suddenly they were faced with a wire fence. Lady Hilton was riding a horse called Cock Robin and Ned was on one called Billy. 'Does mine jump wire?' she called back to Ned. Neither horse had before, but before Ned could answer, she had jumped and he had followed.

'Well, they do now!' he said, and on they galloped from Ballinagar all the way to Ballyneety. The rest of the mounted field, having gone a safer way round, caught up three-quarters of an hour later. 'She was a woman and a half,' Ned recalls.

Another time, with Lord Daresbury, hunting the hounds in his own inimitable way as usual, Ned was on 'a slow old horse' called Bosshot. Hounds found and soon were screaming away; a great hunt across the Limerick countryside was in prospect.

Lady Daresbury was alongside Ned as they approached a bank and ditch.

'After you, M'lady.'

Ned drew Bosshot to one side to allow Lady Daresbury through. She jumped the bank, turned left and headed over the drain, but the grass was long, leaving part of the ditch blind. Both her horse's front legs plunged down into it, sending her over his head with him following, landing on top of her. Her neck was broken and she died instantly. Ned took off his jacket and laid it over her. Someone else rode off to fetch Lord Daresbury. Ned lined himself in front of the casualty as he walked towards her ladyship's husband. But he didn't fool the famous master and huntsman, who took one look at Ned and said, 'She's fucking dead, isn't she?' He drew the hunting horn he was carrying up in front of him: 'She gave me this for Christmas.' And with that he hurled the horn into the ground, turned on his heel and walked away. Unbelievably, she was the second wife he had lost in a hunting accident.

Apart from hunting, Lord Harrington also produced showjumpers who went on to become world renowned. They were 'made' initially in the hunting field, and who else but Ned Kinane was the horseman on top. These included two greys, called The Rock and Rocket, both sold to Raimondo D'Inzeo, and the immortal Irish showjumper Goodbye, brought to fame by Seamus Hayes. Ned's brother Jim also played a part, for while Ned gave Goodbye his early hunting experience it was Jim who first introduced him to showjumping, winning a competition in

Cork as a young man.

Ned worked for Bob Lanigan at Tullamaine Castle for seven or eight years with mares and foals and producing yearlings for the sales in Newmarket and Dublin. His main spell working with Tommy came from Crohane where he still lives. It was an ideal location for training, and the brothers produced a number of successful horses over the years. There were some good horses. One of the best was Smoke Charger, which a number of Ned's nephews rode.

Today, Ned lives in his neat bungalow on top of the hill at Crohane beside the yard where he helped his brother Tommy for so many years, surrounded by photographs of his immediate and wider family.

3

'We want to be jump jockeys!'

Tommy's sons

'**O**h, God, I think I've killed him!' The normally calm Tommy turned to his younger brother Ned and looked on in horror as the thorough-bred racehorse ran away down the road in Holy Cross with his second son Mick on his back. Mick was only nine years old and was being comprehensively 'carted'. Tommy and Ned set off in steady pursuit, anxious not to push the runaway further. The young lad was out of sight by this time. On and on they followed, for about 1½ miles – when there, as they turned a corner, were Mick and horse gently hacking back towards them, Mick relaxed, with his hands dropped and the reins loose, completely unconcerned.

Mick could be a cheeky, happy-go-lucky devil as a young-ster, with a buoyant sense of humour. One day, when they were living in Powerstown Park, Tommy and Frances cycled off to Clonmel to do the weekly shop, leaving Ned in charge of the boys. Thomas was about four or five and Mick only two or three. Ned was pottering around, half an eye on the children playing, half an eye on whatever task was in hand. After a while he realised he could no longer see Mick. He began looking around but still couldn't find him. He opened the coalhouse door and peered in – it was pitch black. He was about to close the door again when suddenly he noticed a pair of white eyes staring at him out of a face completely covered in black coal dust. How on earth was he going to get him cleaned up before Tommy and Frances returned home? Ned told Mick to stay by the back door while he heated kettles and saucepans on the range. Once he had enough he stripped Mick and put him in a bucket of hot water. He scrubbed him until every trace of black had gone and got him dried and dressed in the nick of time before the boy's parents returned.

At bedtime, Mick was often the one to be too alert to go to sleep. Sometimes Ned would look up and see Mick's face peering through the banisters, not wanting to miss anything going on downstairs.

Thomas and Mick began their riding and hunting on the farm pony, a grey called Rocky, but from a young age both were wangling rides on the racehorses. They would run the mile and a half up to the gallops so that they could be allowed to ride the horses home after they had worked. Mick also enjoyed showjumping more than his father, thanks to a pony found by his uncle Michael, which they named Crohane after the home place. The pair notched up numerous wins in the early 1970s when Mick was still a schoolboy, and he also jumped on the hallowed Ballsbridge turf at Ireland's premier horseshow at the Royal Dublin Society.

At about the same time, when he was twelve, Mick tasted racing for the first time. This was a local fun event in Barry's Farm near Lismolin, County Tipperary, and was not one of the more competitive weekly events held for thoroughbreds. Mick was twelve, and the pony was owned by Pat Ryan of Fethard, a whipper-in to the Tipperary Foxhounds. It was the only pony race he ever contested. The outcome was that Mick began his racing career the way he was to continue: by winning.

Boxing was also a part of their childhood for all three older boys, and they won many county and province titles between them. Encouraged by Tommy, Thomas and Mick would practise sparring in the kitchen. Because he was oldest, Thomas was expected to 'go easy' on Mick – but there were times when Thomas saw the competitive glint in Mick's eye and knew he was in for a pasting.

James Kevin was born fewer than twelve months after Mick and was a very small and slight child. From the age of three until four and a half, he lived in the UK with his aunt Maureen and uncle Ned. It was Mick who, as a toddler, introduced his baby brother to some neighbours. His attempt at saying James came out as 'Jayo', and the name stuck. Jayo was musical, and he and Mick played a button accordion. Jayo also played guitar (and still does) and fiddle, while Mick also played a tin whistle as a boy.

Because Thomas and Mick spent their early years together it is easy to forget that actually it is Mick and Jayo who are closest in age. As children, it was Thomas and Mick who went off riding and hunting together, mucking out stables and riding the racehorses. It was Jayo who saw to the farm work, feeding the cattle, hoeing, carting hay and so on. He just wasn't expected to ride and so he didn't.

After Thomas and Mick had outgrown Rocky, the pony was turned away on the farm for a number of years. He had done a good job, pulling the trap with the bales of hay in the summer and hunting during the winter weekends, but when the older boys moved on to racehorses Rocky was made redundant. One day, when Jayo was twelve or thirteen, he told his dad he would like to bring Rocky in and begin riding. His elder brothers had a head start on him, and Tommy was too busy to help Jayo – his own riding career was burgeoning and he was training and farming as well – so Jayo visited his aunt Nancy, Michael's wife, and asked her to teach him to ride on the quiet. Jayo remembers Rocky as 'wider than he was high – he was like a barrel' and able to go at 'about minus one mile per hour'.

Jayo 'just went off hunting', and that was where he learnt to jump – indeed, really to ride, not only obtaining a good seat but also acquiring perfect hands too. Jayo fell off many times at first, but there was always someone there willing to help, to encourage, to nurture. He remembers with fondness the wonderful people in the hunting field who took him under their wing and helped him along: the Ponsonbys, the Croome-Carrolls, the Ronans – 'all lovely people' – and especially the Tipperary Fox-hounds huntsman Michael Higgins – 'no nicer gentleman'.

Jayo recalls attempting to reach the other side of the huge drains that dot the Tipperary landscape: 'Rocky had no scope. He was just a big bundle, but he would burst his way through half a ditch then sit on his backside and slide down the rest like a goat – somehow or other he always got me home.'

One weekend there was to be a meet in Killenaule. All Jayo's schoolfriends would be there, and, apart from that, it was the meet closest to home so he wanted to do his best to have Rocky beautifully turned out. He got the pony as white as snow the night before and put some clean straw down. Sure, didn't he look grand, his kind old face looking out, his lower lip dropped and relaxed, as Jayo went into the house to clean his tack and polish his boots.

Jayo was up early next morning to add the finishing touches: he dusted Rocky's tail with talcum powder to make it even whiter, oiled his hooves so that they were gleaming and tacked him up. He slid over the top and bottom bolts of the stable door and went back indoors to change. But when he went back out Rocky wasn't there. He had kicked the bottom bolt loose, opened the top one with his teeth and let himself out. Worse than that, he had found the deepest, blackest patch of mud to roll in.

Rocky had one other role when the children – the girls as

well – were young. They hung ropes from the girders in the barn and used to play cowboys and Indians off him – swinging on the ropes and trying to knock his riders off.

After Rocky, Jayo, now fourteen, moved on to a black three-quarter-bred eventer that Tommy had bought: Goodman Friday. The talented horse had previously jumped a clear round at Stoneleigh for the Northern Irish (junior) eventing team but he had become difficult – as in he 'would run away with the twelve apostles'. Could the Kinane touch be the key to him?

Although Jayo had come late to riding, and Rocky was diametrically opposite to this new one, he had nevertheless already shown good hands and 'empathy' with horses. The answer was an emphatic yes, and, with Goodman Friday, Jayo experienced the huge reward of transforming a difficult horse and the sheer thrill of riding a good one. Together they went hunting and eventing, and no country was too large for them to cross. Goodman Friday taught Jayo what not to do. Instead of fighting him, Jayo sat still and quietly on him. 'He was so fast and quick, and yet he was like a ballet dancer at the big solid fences.'

From secretly learning to ride on the barrel-like pony with a top speed of 'minus one' to handling the talented but sharp Goodman Friday, it is no surprise that Jayo had both the determination and horsemanship to succeed in later life as a jump jockey – so long as injury didn't intervene.

Youngest brother Paul was born on 27 March 1967, ten years after Thomas, and from the start he was always his own man. The pony that got Paul going and was to start him off on his lifelong love of hunting was called Twinkle. A dark bay with a white blaze, Twinkle was 'a little whore', according to Thomas, who, if her rider fell off, would kick him while on the ground – but she could jump anything. Being so much younger than his brothers, Paul was impatient to be like them and do the things that they did, like jumping the birch schooling fences. Although strictly forbidden, he jumped them on Twinkle and, when challenged by Thomas and Mick, denied it, little knowing that his brothers had watched him through a hole in a hedge.

He was taken in hand out hunting by Tipperary whip and later huntsman Pat Ryan (who had provided the pony that Mick won on in the local pony race). Pat would give him a job out hunting to keep him busy, and Paul and Twinkle would jump anything that got in the way. It is just the same today, and there is nothing Paul loves more than jumping big fences out hunting.

Tommy's daughters

When Frances Kinane discovered in 1973 that she was pregnant for a seventh time, it was, to say the least, a surprise. She had had to spend most of the nine months in bed but what happened the night she went into labour was nightmarish beyond imagination. Tommy remembers, 'It was the biggest storm Ireland had had in living memory.' On Friday, 11 January 1974, the weather was foul, and when Tommy returned home from a farmer's meeting in Tipperary at about 11 p.m., he said, 'A dog wouldn't put out its mother tonight.'

'Looks like you'll have to go out again,' Frances replied.

Frances's sister Margaret came with them for the journey to Tipperary Hospital. They had driven about 10 miles when, 2 miles from Cashel, the road was blocked by fallen trees. Tommy reversed and got into Cashel another way and headed out on the Golden road. This was blocked, Tommy says, by fifteen fallen trees, so they took the road out to the old school at Ballinahinch, but another big tree was across the road there. Next Tommy took a back road (which he knew well, having grown up there) and crossed a bridge but got no further because this time telegraph poles and wires were across the road. By this time, unbeknownst to them, the fire brigade was out looking for them, but they had got stuck as well. Meanwhile, Tommy tried another route by Ardmayle (blocked) and, turning right by Ardmayle bridge, managed to get back into Cashel, where he drove to their family doctor's house. It was now 3 a.m.

'The doctor was drunk, but in those days we had to have a doctor to go into a hospital, so I took him by the back of the neck and put him in the car.' They got Frances to Cashel Hospital for the night, and the next morning an ambulance managed to get her to the maternity ward at Tipperary Hospital. Tommy, meanwhile, was low on petrol – and 1974 was the time of petrol strikes. The petrol station at Kilfeacle Hill refused him any so he got back to Cashel where he paid £1 for some fuel. The hill outside Killenaule was by now blocked by another fallen tree so Tommy abandoned the car and walked over the mountain and down to Crohane, to be greeted in the early morning light by the

Kinane: A Remarkable Racing Family

sight of his sons feeding the cattle for him. Susan and Kathryn, who also helped on the farm, were hoping and praying that they would have a sister.

For Tommy, it was a quick breakfast, a walk back down the mountain to pick up the car, and, with the road now cleared, on he drove to Tipperary, where, that afternoon, Frances gave birth to a daughter. They named her Janette Gale.

None of the girls went into horses (although they all rode ponies as children), but they did learn to box. What's more, when it came to working on the farm they were as good as the boys. Susan, her father said, could carry two heavy bales at a time on her shoulders. She moved to West London and became an award-winning hairdresser, a craft she learnt from her cousin Con, who was a barber in Slough. She now lives in East Anglia with her prison-officer husband Mark and their two children.

Kathryn lives in Naas, where she works for the AIB and sometimes pops in to her father at lunchtime. She acted as almost a second mum to Janette, and at the time Tommy and family moved to the Curragh her younger sister lived with her for three years. She is married to Stephen Burke, who works in sales locally, and the couple have two children.

When Janette left school she planned to study equine science and began with some work experience in the Irish Equine Centre just outside Naas at Johnstown. Before going to college she decided to visit New York, intending to stay a couple of months, but she ended up remaining there for three years. One of the people she met there was her cousin from Connecticut,

Cathy, daughter of Jack, the twenty-years-older brother Tommy Kinane never met. When she returned she knew for sure that it was a degree in equine science that she wanted. She qualified at Limerick and now works back where she started, in the Irish Equine Centre. She is married to car salesman Mark Kennedy, and they live in Sallins, with their son and daughter who was born in 2010.

It is every jump jockey's dream to win the Grand National. Even to ride in it is more than many achieve. Tommy's first of three rides came in 1968 when, at the age of thirty-four, he was in constant demand in Ireland as a tough, pugnacious, lightweight jockey of great strength. In 1968, Tommy was booked for a 28–1 chance Reynard's Heir, owned by R. Buckley and trained by Leslie Crawford in Northern Ireland. The favourite was the stunning Different Class, good-looking enough to win in the show-ring – his owner's looks, too, were in a different class for he happened to be film star Gregory Peck.

Tommy and Frances stayed in the Holiday Inn but, like most of those involved in the great race, they were sure to visit Liverpool's Adelphi Hotel. The Adelphi has been synonymous with Aintree ever since the first running of the Grand National in 1839; then, like all the other hotels within proximity of the novel new race, there were so many visitors that three or four

Kinane: A Remarkable Racing Family

men slept to a bed. The Edwardian grandeur of the Adelphi has not, over the years, prevented winning National jockeys from swinging from its glistening crystal chandeliers or from getting up to other pranks.

Tommy was a senior jockey, though his best day still lay more than a decade ahead. He looked around him. Among other Irish jockeys rubbing shoulders that year were Eddie Harty (Steel Bridge), Barry Brogan (second on Moidore's Token), Owen McNally on Highland Wedding (who was to win the following year for Eddie Harty), Tommy Carberry (Great Lark), John Harty (Ronald's Boy), E. Prendergast (Valouis) and amateur Billy McLernon (Forecastle). The jockey who fielded most publicity was sixty-eight-year-old American amateur Tim Durant. Another hardy amateur in the line-up was John Ciechanowski, while at the other end of the scale teenager Nigel Thorne was riding the mare Polaris Missile. At seventeen, Thorne was already a promising amateur.

It was the era of 'last Grand Nationals', and, according to the press, the course would shortly be developed for housing. Tommy walked the course, the size of the fences dwarfing him, but after the hunting fields of Tipperary they didn't daunt him. The trickle of spectators arriving turned to a throng so that by the time of the 'off' a huge crowd packed the stands.

Back home in Farney Castle, it was left to Thomas and Mick to do the mundane mucking out at home. The two excited little boys got up early to get on with the chores. It was so cold and frosty that Thomas's hands stuck to the USA blue assortment biscuit tin containing their packed lunch when he carried it, and, try as he might, he could not make the 'granny bike' with a cog missing go any faster. Perhaps that was just as well because Mick, two years his junior, was still on a child's bike and only just about able to keep up.

Of all the jobs with horses, mucking out is probably the only one guaranteed to warm you up, and before too long the young fellas were cycling home again and dashing round to the pub. The Gormans, who ran it, were good friends as well as neighbours of the Kinanes and didn't blink at letting the youngsters in, proceeding through the shop to the bar at the back where there was a black-and-white television. The men holding beers and smoking roll-ups parted to let Thomas and Mick into the front, not only because they were small but also because their father, the local hero, was taking part in the race on the small screen.

Over in Aintree, Tommy cantered the eight-year-old Reynard's Heir down to show him the first fence and then joined the interminable circling at the start with the other forty-four horses in front of the packed stand, the spectators wondering if they were to witness another winner like Foinavon the previous year when a loose horse had caused such carnage at the fence after Becher's that Foinavon and his jockey John Buckingham alone had jumped it at the first attempt.

The tape flew up, and the horses galloped down the formidable long line of fences. Number six was Becher's Brook, and six fell there. At Gorman's pub in Holy Cross Thomas and Mick peered at the grainy screen searching: there, on the inside where the drops are steepest – 'the brave man's route' – was their father, enjoying a dream ride. Even to their young eyes they could see the horse was 'jumping for fun', and they began jumping up and down excitedly, their fists flailing imaginary whips, their voices yelling, 'Come on, Dad!'

Up front, Red Alligator and his twenty-year-old pilot Brian Fletcher drew away from Moidore's Token and Different Class. Another 'Red' was to come into the winning rider's life a few short years later: Brian Fletcher rode Red Rum to the first two of his record-breaking three victories.

The boys watched agog, cheering each time they picked out their dad on the fuzzy screen and urging him on. They tried to count the horses as they passed the post, led by a long way by Red Alligator and then, close up together, Moidore's Token and Different Class, followed by Rutherfords and The Fossa. Another bunch followed, six, seven, eight. Tommy was among those, and there were another ten or so horses strung out behind. Reynard's Heir finished a creditable official eighth of seventeen to get round.

The two lads turned and looked at each other. There was only one future for them. Thomas and Mick both knew that they wanted to be jockeys. Jump jockeys, of course.

Polaris Missile was one of those to fall at Becher's first time, but her youthful rider was quick to pick himself up and remount, eventually pulling up. A year later, young Nigel Thorne was killed in a car crash when returning from a day's drag-hunting. A dozen years later, in 1981, Nigel's father John rode Polaris Missile's son Spartan Missile in the Grand National, and, having lost his stirrup irons, the fifty-four-year-old amateur finished a gallant second to Aldaniti and Bob Champion. The following spring, John himself was killed in a point-to-point fall.

Tommy Kinane's next visit to the bleak site that sets the Liverpool suburbs alight for three days each April was in 1973, and this time he was paid 'danger' money to persuade him to take the ride on a horse that the trainer knew 'wasn't able for it'. As often happens, the owner simply wanted a runner in the great race and was not for dissuading. Tommy met the trainer, none other than Arkle's redoubtable rider Pat Taaffe, in the Adelphi Hotel. Pat had coaxed 'a good few quid' for the jockey from the owners, the jewellers H. Samuel, and, as the delectable sweet trolley came around at the end of the meal, Tommy joked to the waitress, 'Bring me a bucket and I'll have them all.' The horse was Beggar's Way, a nine-year-old set to carry 10 stone 1 pound that started at 33–1. As predicted, he duly fell. Tommy recalls, 'It was Becher's Brook first time round: he just galloped into it and fell downwards in a straight line as if he'd been shot.'

The Indian rubber ball that is Tommy Kinane picked himself up and caught hold of one of the loose horses. There was a television screen relaying the race to spectators near Becher's, and Tommy watched and listened from there as one of the greatest of Grand Nationals unfolded. Blazing a trail and jumping the great fences as if they were 'upturned dandy brushes' was the mighty Australian horse Crisp. He galloped and jumped his way further and further into a lead perhaps only before seen by Troytown in 1920. That year, Troytown's only danger had been when, in appalling ground, he demolished the twenty-sixth fence. For the gallant Crisp and his intrepid rider Richard Pitman, the danger that loomed was one horse who managed to detach himself from the remaining toiling field and set off in pursuit up that long, long run-in. Crisp was shouldering a top weight of 12 stone. The upstart pursuing him, ridden by Brian Fletcher, was on 10.5. Barely a stride before the winning post he passed the long-time leader to win. His name was Red Rum. It was a tear-jerking performance.

Interestingly, the pair had started at 9–1 joint favourites. L'Escargot, the dual Gold Cup winner whose turn was eventually to come in 1975, was third. He was also on 12 stone and was next in the market. Crisp did not run in the Grand National again, but the quality of that epic race is franked by the 'also rans' such as L'Escargot and, in particular, Red Rum himself, who went on to win again the following year, to finish runner-up in both 1975 and 1976 and, historically, to win a record third time in 1977.

Tommy Kinane was back for another attempt in 1974, and he harboured hopes for the eleven-year-old Pearl of Montreal, for all his 50–1 starting price. As usual he was riding at a low weight, this time the minimum of 10 stone. On the morning of the race he walked the course with his mount's trainer, Larry Greene. Red Rum was in again, but this time he was set to carry the top weight of 12 stone, one pound more than L'Escargot.

The forty-two runners set off on perfect ground, and soon Tommy was experiencing one of steeplechasing's greatest thrills: he was right up in the vanguard on Pearl of Montreal, enjoying a spectacular ride in the front ranks and jumping perfectly. Becher's Brook, tightly round the Canal Turn, Valentine's and then, approaching the stands, the biggest fence on the course, the Chair – all fine. They are over the water and heading off down that long line of fences away into the country again. Becher's once more, the Canal Turn and now approaching Valentine's for the last time. Family and friends held their collective breaths as the pair jumped jointly into the lead. Here was a real chance of winning the world's greatest race, with only five more fences and that infamous long run in to negotiate.

Then, in a couple of strides, Pearl of Montreal 'went out like a light'. Disappointed, hardly believing it, Tommy pulled him up and at once saw the reason: blood was pouring from the horse's nostril. He had broken a blood vessel. It is one of those things that may never show up in work at home but under the greater pressure of a race it can, and, once a horse has a tendency, the bleeding can happen again. In America, horses are allowed to run on medication called Lasix for it, but in the UK and Ireland drugs are banned so all horses run showing their true physical worth.

Tommy could only hack quietly back. Meanwhile, it was once again Red Rum, this time truly proving his worth under top weight, who beat L'Escargot, Charles Dickens and Spanish Steps.

4

The coalman's horse and others

When Tommy moved to Crohane from Farney Castle he bought a trailer off a neighbour, Tommy Wade, and transported his wife and six children, and his furniture, in relays. (Wade was the rider of one of Ireland's greatest-ever showjumpers, Dundrum, which Thomas can remember riding on the road when he was seven.) The thatched house was set on top of a steep hill and provided an ideal setting for training racehorses. It was the beginning of twenty memorable years there, including the start of all four sons' racing careers.

For the first ten years Tommy concentrated on his riding career with considerable success, and he also farmed. He rented a further 150 acres and built up a suckler herd of 150 head. It was a far cry from his original one cow and a red calf and no tractor, when he first bought a house while working for his brother Dan.

Tragedy struck the farm in the early 1980s: the herd went down with brucellosis, and every single animal had to be destroyed. There was scant compensation in those days, and the banks charged 24 per cent interest on loans when Tommy was buying replacements, but he restarted from scratch and built up the herd once more. Luckily, on the racecourse, the winners were coming thick and fast, and, now in his thirties, his best was still to come.

Tommy Kinane rode for every Irish trainer bar one during his career – north, south, east and west – a testament to his popularity as one of the strongest lightweight jump jockeys of his generation. The only exception was Tom Dreaper, who, with six jockeys of his own, including amateurs, never needed to call on Tommy's services.

Listowel was a happy hunting ground for Tommy. The Kerry track, situated across the river Feale from the town centre, hosts its feature harvest festival meeting each September. It has become so popular that it now extends to seven days, with a festival flavour that permeates throughout the town. Its centrepiece is the Kerry National, a race that has itself produced future Aintree Grand National winners such as Monty's Pass. Tommy himself won it twice, first in 1973, riding Pearl of Montreal, trained by Larry Greene. The gelding had won it in 1971 when trained by Paddy Sleator on a weight of 10 stone 12 pounds. He had dropped right down in the handicap two years later, and who better than Tommy Kinane for a 9 stone 7 pounds ride to give owner G. F. F. Fasenfeld his second win in the race. Pearl of Montreal won a number of other good chases, too, including in Leopardstown and Fairyhouse, and was the horse on whom Tommy had the last of his three rides in the Aintree Grand National.

Tommy's second Kerry National win came the following year on board Irishman for trainer Archie Watson. In the same year, 1974, Tommy, already more than forty years old, won the Troytown Chase in Navan on Cottage King (yet another 9-stone-7-pound winner for the 'veteran lightweight'), trained by C. McCartan Junior for Mrs N. Mulcair.

During his riding career, Tommy rode as first jockey to both Leslie Crawford, a respected steward in Northern Ireland, and to Willie Deacon in Wexford, a man with an equally fine, upright reputation. One year, Tommy had a great ride in the Stayers Hurdle, now known as the World Hurdle, at the Cheltenham Festival. Riding the Willie Deacon-trained mare Clonroche, he finished a good third. Her daughter, Clonroche Lady, trained in Ireland by J. A. O'Connell, was to win a maiden hurdle in Fairyhouse at odds of 25–1 in 1974.

For Leslie Crawford, Tommy rode a kinky horse called Razor's Edge, who won good-class hurdle races in Listowel, Leopardstown and Liverpool. Tommy also won for the same trainer in Navan on a horse called Dark Concern on a Saturday, and the following Wednesday the horse turned out to win again in Leopardstown before the handicapper caught up with him. He must have been a tough, sound horse, for in the 1978–9 season, when trained by James Murphy for owner Miss M. Cotter, he ran fifteen times and gained one win and five second placings.

Another Leslie Crawford horse was War Bonnet, with whom Tommy went over to Wetherby, Yorkshire, to ride in a Wills Premier Chase qualifier. Tommy had a nasty dose of flu, but no one watching could have guessed. In the race Tommy tracked the favourite, Ben More, and found it difficult to peg him back – 'so I drove the horse so hard to the last that I never saw the fence.' Tommy's bravery was rewarded with a win, and afterwards Fred Winter was heard to ask who was that jockey, Tommy Kinane.

Tommy and War Bonnet ventured across the water again to finish a gallant fourth to the same horse in the final at Haydock, with the favourite Tamalin third. Another gentleman of Irish racing for whom he rode was Paddy Sleator, winning the Easter Chase, Fairyhouse, on Artistic Prince, carrying the now customary big-race low weight of 9 stones 7 pounds.

Michael Cunningham was another noted trainer for whom he won, along with Tom Costello, who died in 2009, and who is best remembered for producing no fewer than six individual Cheltenham Gold Cup winners from his County Clare acres, Best Mate included.

One of Tommy's best rides came in the 1967 Scottish Grand National on board Reynard's Heir, who he also rode in the premier Aintree event. 'I thought Reynard's Heir might win the next year's Grand National, but he broke down,' Tommy recalls. In 1967, up at Ayr, he was beaten a short head in a rousing finish by The Fossa, ridden by Andy Turnell. The Fossa finished fourth in the 1967 Aintree feature, fifth the next year and ran in it a total of five times.

A few weeks before the Scottish event Tommy almost had a double reason to celebrate: on the day of the birth of his son, Paul, on 27 March 1967, he came tantalisingly close to winning the Irish Grand National, but Reynard's Heir was beaten into second by the Paddy Mullins-trained Vulpine.

It was in 1977 that Tommy first took out a trainer's licence in his own name, although, as we have seen, he had trained privately for the licence holders at both Clonmel and Holy Cross. He started off on his own account in Crohane with ten or twelve horses and continued to race ride. The first horse that he trained from there was a grey filly called Sidon Star belonging to Dundrum butcher Paddy Hennessy. The two-year-old grey was bred by Anne Biddle from Naas, and the flying filly provided Tommy with his first official training win, at Limerick. She was ridden by his son Mick.

Mick Kinane was riding her again in Limerick Junction while Tommy was up in County Mayo at the attractive summer course of Ballinrobe to ride a horse there. It was June, and the horse Tommy was riding, Paddy Tudor, was having its twentieth start of the season, but neither that fact nor its 7-pound penalty for its most recent win affected the seven-year-old. Battling gamely and with the trademark strong assistance from the saddle, he won by a head for owner-trainer Bill Durkhan. Tommy didn't wait to celebrate; instead, he weighed in and dashed to his car, still wearing his breeches and boots, and headed diagonally across Ireland as fast as his Ford could take him.

Meanwhile, at Limerick Junction, eldest son Thomas legged his brother Mick into Sidon Star's saddle. At home, Thomas groomed Sidon Star as he was the only one who could handle her; she would kick out at other lads and send them running out of her stable in fright. Now Thomas told Mick he thought she would win again. Mick replied that there was a very big two-year-old likely to beat them.

Tommy screeched into the car park and ran across to the enclosure just in time to hear the commentator announce the result: the filly had indeed been beaten by the big horse. Tommy, still in his breeches, reached the unsaddling enclosure in time to greet Mick as he rode Sidon Star into the berth reserved for the horse placed second.

It is no surprise that the sort of horses Tommy was sent to train were the difficult ones, ones that others couldn't handle. They could be rewarding when they were 'got right', but they were unlikely to lead to classier, more lucrative racing recruits being sent his way. He had already trained one such for Michael Purcell at Farney Castle. The horse was owned by the local coalman and was called, perhaps appropriately, Shoot. He had been given away by his former trainer Willie Treacy, and Tommy set about seeing what he could do with him. The problem was that he was a tearaway: he would sweat up profusely and try to run away in his races. Tommy insisted on riding him himself at home, working him alone and trying to calm him down.

He was soon showing considerable ability when cantering, and Tommy wasted down to 9 stone in order to take the ride on him himself in a 1-mile-1-furlong flat race in Tramore. It was a tape start, and Tommy jumped out first, got him to settle in front, and won, beating the favourite, without the other runners ever getting close to him. When Tommy moved on from Farney Castle, the horse went to Paddy Sleator, where it was discovered that Shoot suffered from a heart murmur; nevertheless, he went on to become a top showjumper in Switzerland.

All four of Tommy's sons rode for him at various times, and a number of his nephews, too. Tommy achieved his ambition of training a Cheltenham runner when Cherryfield was beaten by only a head at the October meeting having been almost brought down three fences out. He had previously won by twenty lengths at Carlisle, carrying 12 stone 2 pounds and ridden by Jayo. Tommy also had a few runners at Aintree (though not in the Grand National), with Born to Shine, ridden by Thomas, and Champagne Brigade.

In 1989, after twenty years at Crohane, Mick persuaded his parents Tommy and Frances to move up to the Curragh. There, they built a house near Mick's Clunemore Lodge and named it Knockavilla, after Frances' home parish in Tipperary. Tommy built a neat yard and continued to train for another ten years. The couple had lived in Tipperary all their lives (bar the brief period in England), but they soon felt at home in Ireland's racing headquarters.

5

Cheltenham calls

Monksfield

In the mid-1970s, a tough little horse with a huge heart came along to provide the crowning glory of Tommy's riding career and to kick-start that of his son, Mick. Monksfield also boosted the training career of Des McDonogh, tucked away in the northern tip of County Meath, who at the time, in his words, 'had a yard full of empty boxes'.

His son, Declan, a champion Irish flat jockey today, was not yet born, but in his wife Helen (née Bryce-Smith) Des had a 'right-hand man' of the highest calibre. A top-class point-to-point rider in those days, she still cuts a dash crossing the Meath countryside behind a pack of hounds.

Monksfield himself spawned one of those fairytale stories: the produce of a chance mating by Gala Performance out of a Tulyar mare and an unusual sale, he was lucky to find his way to a small, informal yard where he could be given individual time and attention. Not for him a case of being number 90 in the bottom yard of a 100-horse stable – well cared for as such horses are, they are unlikely to become 'part of the family' as was Monksfield's good fortune.

What struck me most when I visited him at the McDonogh's at the end of his career was that Monksfield didn't look particularly small, probably because he was built in perfect proportion. But, as a two-year-old, he was both small and unfurnished (not yet filled out), and, much as he needed to, Des had been unable to sell him on. An all-too-rare winner changed that when an Irish Canadian radiologist, Dr Michael Mangan, was introduced to the McDonoghs in the winner's enclosure, liked the young couple and asked if they happened to have a horse for sale. The rest, as they say, is history.

A 'rookie' owner, Dr Mangan had the wise good sense not to interfere with the trainer's plans, to listen to his advice and, above all, to have patience. That patience meant just one 'educational' run as a two-year-old shortly before the end of the season in October 1974. Monksfield, however, had other ideas, and, to the astonishment of everyone, including his devoted young trainer, he 'hacked up' at 25–1, paying 647–1 on the Tote. In one of those awful quirks of racing, the McDonoghs' other runner of the day, a recent novice-chase winner, was killed in a later race.

The following year, Monksfield ran in a number of flat races and placed a few times without winning again. Had he been in a big yard at this time it is quite possible he might have been gelded – and very likely not heard of again. He remained, however, an 'entire' and, as such, showed a bullish love of racing and that intangible quality: the will to win.

So it was that in November 1975 he made his debut over hurdles, Helen having found him a 'natural' in schooling. He started his hurdling career in the same way as on the flat: by winning. In another cruel twist, the McDonoghs lost one of his fellow stable inmates that night, 22 November, from a twisted gut.

After a few more hurdle runs which included another win, it was time to put Monksfield against older horses in a handicap. In spite of his success in novice company, he was allotted only 9 stone 7 pounds in his second handicap, a weight that not many established senior jockeys could 'do'. Enter Tommy Kinane. It was 24 January 1976, at Naas, when Tommy's partnership with the four-year-old colt began. Tommy had previously ridden occasionally for Helen's parents, and, according to Helen's formidable mother, Jean Bryce-Smith, Tommy 'was utterly fearless, a bit dashing as a jockey. He always went straight to the front whatever you told him to do. He was a character, a rough-and-tumble jockey, you know; as hard as he could go, as fast as he could go for as long as he could go.'[*]

---

[*] Jonathan Powell (1980) *Monksfield*, Tadworth: World's Work, p. 52.

Ten runners lined up for the 2-mile event, and Tommy was instructed to hold up Monksfield and to come with a strong run to lead at the last flight. Obeying orders, he so nearly succeeded in winning. The Jim Dreaper-trained Straight Row, carrying 11 stones 2 pounds, and ridden by Tommy Carberry, beat them by a head, with the favourite four lengths back. Tommy remembers it well: 'Monksfield jumped like a buck, and I didn't give him a hard race.'

The horse had run a blinder against established horses very early in his fourth year. He was a June foal, which is late even for a National Hunt horse and meant he was probably a number of months younger than his rivals (all thoroughbreds having their official birthday on 1 January). He had more weight on his back for his next run, and so it was back to Frank Berry as rider, finishing fifth of fifteen, before Tommy once more had the leg-up, carrying 9 stones 12 pounds, in a handicap at Fairyhouse.

The instructions were the same as before, and once more the pair were beaten by a head, this time by the Dan Moore-trained Bedwell Prince carrying only 9 stones 4 pounds. It was becoming clear that while Monksfield had the speed for 2 miles he also had excellent stamina, and Tommy remains convinced that had he been allowed to make more use of the colt that day he would have won.

They did not have too much longer to wait. At Navan, in March, Monksfield was allotted 10 stones 7 pounds, but Tommy retained the ride; he was to become the jockey who rode the little horse more times than any other. Their strength, determination and battling qualities suited each other.

Des McDonogh's father had just died, and so it was Helen who not only saddled up Monksfield but also sewed black armbands onto the white sleeves of his colours. Monksfield had been showing signs of courage and willingness in his previous runs. Now he was about to display the sort of gutsiness that marked him out in a manner that in the next decade would belong to the mare Dawn Run.

There were eleven runners, and it was by far the toughest race for the youngster so far, both during the early part, with plentiful jostling, and over the last half mile where one horse after another came to challenge. He pinned back his ears, dug deep and fended them off to beat the favourite by three-quarters of a length with the same distance back to the third horse.

It was proof, if proof were needed, that here was a horse who could be a serious contender in Cheltenham's four-year-old championship, the Daily Express Triumph Hurdle. Always run with a big field full of hopefuls, it is invariably the metaphorical graveyard of many. Fine reputations can be shattered, and even the winner may never be heard of again. It can take so much out of a youngster. Equally, the winner will often become favourite for the following year's Champion Hurdle. Significantly, it can be the runner-up who goes on to the highest honours.

Twelve days after their Navan victory, Tommy and Monksfield lined up for the 1976 Triumph, the curtain-raiser to the great Cheltenham Festival: the pinnacle of the National Hunt season, keenly contested from across both the Irish Sea and the

English Channel. The 'big three' championship jump races are the Champion Hurdle, the Queen Mother Two Mile Champion Chase and the Cheltenham Gold Cup, run over an extended 3 miles.

Now, in March 1976, Tommy was to ride in the Triumph Hurdle, the championship test for four-year-olds. The Champion Hurdle would follow a year later, but the third and greatest of the big three, the Cheltenham Gold Cup, never came his way.

By this stage Tommy was riding very short and had earned a reputation for great power in the saddle. His son, Thomas, says he learnt by watching how his father could be niggling away at a horse totally unseen by his rivals, an attribute that enabled him to pounce on the unwary on more than one occasion.

There were twenty-three runners of such a high class that Monksfield, despite his successes, was out at 28–1 in price. He didn't know that, of course, and for forty-three-year-old Tommy Kinane it was a huge opportunity at an age when most National Hunt jockeys have long since retired.

Now the runners came under starter's orders. Little could Tommy Kinane or the racing public know that they were about to witness the first, but not the last, of the controversies surrounding the rider and the super little horse.

Tommy's instructions were to give the horse a chance early on, to close up down the hill and to keep enough in reserve for the tough run to the line. As always, the juveniles set off at a furious pace so that before long the pair was struggling just to keep tabs on the main group, round the bend and up the far hill. But as they swept downhill, Monksfield and a few others went in hot pursuit of the long-time leader, John Bryce-Smith's mare Mwanadike. Monksfield was on the outside when the leader hung right-handed, carrying him with her. For a moment it looked as if the Irish pair (trained by brothers-in-law) would both be out of the race. They straightened up in time, and Monksfield headed for the last flight almost in line with Mwanadike and Peterhof, with the favourite Prominent King close behind.

Tommy was in the sort of battle he relished, and he had a willing accomplice. Raising his whip hand, he conjured a perfect leap from Monksfield to land running, but, as they headed off up the climb to the post, they again found themselves being carried right-handed, this time by Peterhof. Peterhof came right across him, and, although Peterhof won by one and a half lengths, Tommy insisted that an objection be lodged. He was certain he would be awarded the race in the stewards' room, but, to his fury, he was not. Tommy recalls, 'I have no doubt to this day I should have got it in the stewards' room; half as little was done the other day [in the 2010 English 1,000 Guineas] and they lost it in the stewards' room.'

Significantly, the run allowed connections to dream of the coming year – and the 1977 Champion Hurdle.

Monksfield's season was not over yet, however; hardy, bonny and with a constitution seemingly of iron, he thrived on what he was bred to do: race. He was ridden in an apprentice flat race at Naas by sixteen-year-old Mick Kinane. Looking at a picture of him beating the favourite it is clear that even then, riding his third-ever winner, Mick had style, strength and polish. Monksfield and the teenager won this race three years in succession. Monksfield had two more hurdle races, hacking up first at Fairyhouse and then finishing third under a big weight at Punchestown. On this occasion it was none other than Tommy's eighteen-year-old son Thomas who was on board the winner, Multiple, trained by his brother Christy.

The new year of 1977 brought more encouraging performances prior to Monksfield's crack at the Champion Hurdle. Tommy Kinane, at forty-four years of age, was having his first ride in it. Before the race, Tommy and Des walked the course together, noting the gradients and the wet patches. The Champion Hurdle is the level-weighted contest for the world's best hurdlers where speed and accurate jumping are essential if success is to be gained. Trainer and rider talked through tactics for their 15–1 shot. Tommy was asked to hold him up; to this day, he wishes he had been allowed to make more use of the colt.

In the race, fearing he was being boxed in as star horses loomed around him going down the hill – horses such as Sea Pigeon, Birds Nest, Beacon Light, Dramatist and the reigning champion Night Nurse – Tommy pulled Monksfield out around them. Even so, he was the main challenger to Night Nurse at the last flight, and, as usual, Tommy drove his mount hard at it. Unusually, Monksfield made one of only a very few serious jumping mistakes in his life, and, at such a crucial stage, it may have cost him victory, even though he ran on with his trademark courage. He was beaten by two lengths and was a similar distance ahead of the third-placed Dramatist, with Sea Pigeon fourth.

The next day, when the Gold Cup was won by Dessie Hughes riding Davy Lad after the luckless Tied Cottage fell at the last, Tommy had the ride on Kilcoleman in the County Handicap Hurdle. There were twenty-six runners, and his regular rival Mwanadike, 11 stones 8 pounds, was favourite, with Kilcoleman, 10 stones, at 14–1. In an exciting finish, in which Kilcoleman hung badly up the run in, they beat the favourite by three-quarters of a length for the Jimmy Boyers and Pat Clarke team.

Tommy was to ride once in the Champion Chase, finishing fifth on Flashy Boy for trainer Archie Watson from Northern Ireland in 1977, when it was won for the second successive year by Skymas, ridden by Mouse Morris. 'The boys' in the weighing room – jockeys such as Barry Brogan and Bob Champion – said Tommy had no chance of staying on Flashy Boy, trained in later years by Denys Smith. But among Tommy's riding credentials was the ability to stick on like a limpet. His experience in the hunting field made him difficult to dislodge from the saddle. He is critical of today's UK jockeys, who, he says, 'would fall off a soft bed'. 'There is nothing like hunting for making a jockey, and that's why most of the top jockeys in the UK are Irish.'

Tommy headed for Liverpool in bullish form, first for a ride over the big fences on Glenvale Prince in the Topham Trophy and then to partner his little warrior in the Templegate Hurdle. It was not to be. A fall at the third-last in the Topham left Tommy with a kick on his arm. He rode in the next race, but by the next day his arm was so stiff and sore that he could barely move it. 'I was due to ride Artistic Prince and Kintai on the Friday but I stood myself down to make sure I'd be OK for Saturday.'

A combination of painkillers and physio saw him present himself to trainer and owner on Saturday morning, ready to ride Monksfield in the keenly anticipated rematch with Night Nurse later that afternoon. But Monksfield's owner Dr Mangan only wanted a fully fit rider, and he asked Tommy who he might suggest. 'My first choice was Frank Berry but for some reason they didn't want him so then I suggested my friend Dessie Hughes.'

The race that followed, with Mick O'Toole's stable jockey Dessie Hughes in the saddle, goes down in horse-racing annals as one of the finest ever witnessed, on a par with Grundy and Bustino on the flat at Ascot in the July 1975 King George VI and Queen Elizabeth Diamond Stakes (known colloquially as the 'King George'). The Templegate Hurdle at Liverpool, run over 2 miles 5 furlongs (considerably longer than the Champion Hurdle), produced an even closer result: a dead heat between Monksfield and Night Nurse. Tommy says, 'Des told me that I would have won on him, that he was unused to him and got tired. Anyway, I got the ride back the next year.'

Monksfield's season was not yet over. He thrived in the spring, and next he had the middle of his three assignations with Mick Kinane in which he beat Joanna Morgan in the apprentice race at Naas. One more hurdle run under the impossible weight of 12 stones 4 pounds brought a close fourth in Punchestown, ridden again by Dessie Hughes. The tough and durable Monksfield had run in thirteen hurdles and three times on the flat during the season.

The next autumn, Monksfield warmed up on the flat and placed over hurdles before running what Tommy believes to have been one of his career-best races at Fairyhouse in December. The plan for March 1978 was firmly the Champion Hurdle until a debilitating illness intervened, and, for long weeks, Monksfield looked unlikely to reach the racecourse at all. He was off the track for two and a half months, and the prospects for Cheltenham looked worse than forlorn, but once he was over his illness Monksfield celebrated by pulling his trainer's arms out at home, bucking and generally showing a renewed *joie de vivre*.

He was ready for a quiet run in late January, but Dessie Hughes was unavailable so Tommy was booked for his friend once more. He gave him the gentle ride that the recent invalid needed and then kept the mount for the Erin Foods Champion Hurdle in February at Leopardstown and for the Champion Hurdle in March at Cheltenham itself.

Tommy travelled over to his relations in Middlesex and took the coach to Cheltenham along with them and his kit, stopping for breakfast at the Puesdown Inn. It was to turn into the most exciting day of his life. He did more than walk the course before the race: he ran round much of it, including jumping the hurdles himself. Forty-five years old he might be, but no one was going to claim he was unfit. He was in ideal form to ride the race of his life, confident, knowing and fit.

It was a superb Champion Hurdle, with the previous year's winner and runner-up, Night Nurse and Monksfield, sweeping into the lead down the hill; Sea Pigeon was poised not far behind. Tommy, knowing both his horse and the form of the opposition, made his vital move. 'I wanted to make use of his stamina. I knew the others would be queuing up behind ready to pounce. I needed to get first run and so I set sail for home. We flew down the hill, soared over the second-last and were clear so tight on the rail that no one could have got up our inside.'

It was what Tommy had lived his life for: speed, excitement and craftiness. He had the best possible ally in Monksfield, and together they charged towards the final flight. Sea Pigeon, ridden by Frank Berry, was pressing them, but Monksfield put in a superb winning leap and landed running. With only that hill ahead of him the issue was put beyond doubt.

At home in Tipperary, Ned watched the race unfold on television. He would never forget the excitement. Monksfield was a supremely popular and deserving winner, and, for Tommy Kinane, ten years older and more than most of his fellow jumping jockeys, it was truly the crowning moment of his long career.

Tommy had been interviewed for television in the paddock before the race by Julian Wilson. Jauntily, Tommy had told Julian he would be repeating the process in a few minutes' time as he had every intention of being the winner. In fact, that task fell to Derek 'Tommo' Thompson. Tommy hung around only for long enough to buy a crate of champagne and to ask his fellow jockeys Andy Turnell and Jeff King to share it out in the weighing room with the 'boys', taking two bottles himself for his family. He packed his breeches into his bag and set off back in the coach for Ruislip, Middlesex, with his sister Mary and her husband Frank, his sister Alice, her son Con and his wife Eileen and pals from Harefield Irish Club. From there they went out for a celebratory meal in the Orchard Hotel, with Tommy, as usual, sipping no more than orange juice.

A few days later there were further celebrations, with a dinner in the Cashel Palace Hotel for Tommy and Frances, Jayo, Thomas, Ned and Maureen, as well as Des and Helen McDonogh and various neighbours and friends, organised by Monksfield's owner, Dr Mangan.

Just over two weeks later, Tommy looked forward to riding Monksfield at Liverpool, but, just as in the previous year, injury intervened. He took a crashing fall on Kintai in the 1978 Irish Grand National at Fairyhouse on Easter Monday (won by Brown Lad). It was at the regulation (open ditch) where first Mighty's Honour and Tommy Carberry fell, bringing down John Fowler on Credit Card. Kintai appeared distracted, fell and cannoned Tommy headlong into the ground. Being Tommy, he picked himself up, got through the first-aid room, dressed in the jockeys' changing room and drove home to Tipperary where Frances had tea prepared. She took one look at him and drove him straight to Cashel Hospital where for the second time in his career he lay flat on his back for the next eleven weeks.

It was the most frustrating period he can remember. He couldn't bear to think of Monksfield running at Liverpool for the second year without him. He almost fought with the staff and, in his words, threatened to throw the senior nurse out of the window because she wouldn't wheel him to the television. Furious, Tommy was on the point of going home in his pyjamas when Dr Rodney Foxwell, a famous bone specialist from Vancouver, calmed him down. Tommy used to box with Dr Foxwell and remains in touch with his widow, Jane, who he occasionally visits in Vancouver.

At Liverpool, Monksfield, always a spring horse, ran one of his best races and simply cruised past Night Nurse to victory in spite of carrying 5 pounds extra in weight for his Champion win.

That fall should have finished Tommy's career but, not surprisingly, with a carrot like a second Champion Hurdle to look forward to, it did not.

The Champion Hurdle, the world's top hurdling prize, could – *should* – have resulted in a surge of owners wanting a horse with the winner's trainer, but that was slow to happen for Des McDonogh, perhaps because he was not inclined to put himself out in the social scene, preferring to share the stable duties at home. Eventually his success did lead to one new inmate who became significant in the Tommy Kinane story: Stranfield. At the start of the next season, Stranfield was simply another occupant of McDonogh's yard. Monksfield was his star, and Tommy rode him in his first four races of that season, 1978–9, winning first time out at Down Royal when Dessie Hughes was off with a broken ankle. Next time out, Tommy and his old friend failed by the narrowest margin, a short head, to give very nearly 3 stone to Milan Major at Naas. Next up was the Benson and Hedges Handicap Hurdle at Fairyhouse in early December with Monksfield set to carry his now-customary 12 stone. The trainer felt the jockey made too much use of the horse under that weight, ending up in him having too hard a race. Tommy, furious that he was crossed on the run-in, was convinced he would win the race in the stewards' room, but he did not.

It was shortly after this that Des McDonogh, after talking to the owner, approached Dessie Hughes, still in plaster, with a tentative booking for the Champion Hurdle more than three months away. Tommy Kinane did not know about this and gave Monksfield a kind race on his next run, nursing him in heavy ground and a huge weight to finish third in the Sweeps Handicap Hurdle at Leopardstown's Christmas meeting. He had ridden exactly as he had been asked to do.

The new year of 1979 was marked not only by weeks of ice and snow but also by months of a postal and telephone strike. Eventually the weather relented enough to allow Monksfield to run at Leopardstown at the end of February in a much-needed prep race for the Champion Hurdle, as the freeze-up had left him short of peak fitness. Again, the race and the riding of

Monksfield did not pan out the way the trainer wanted. It led to a very public and heated 'discussion' between Des McDonogh and Tommy Kinane outside the weighing room that some reports put as lasting the best part of an hour.

'More like five minutes,' says Tommy. 'I don't remember there being much of a falling out with Des. I had been told to hold him up, but they went at a crawl and ended in a sprint that left him behind. He never liked Leopardstown but, more than that, after the hold-up caused by the weather he was as fat as a brood mare.' Even so, despite reservations about the rider by Monksfield's connections, it was not until one week before the Champion Hurdle when, after consultation with the owner, the young trainer finally told the veteran rider that he was to be replaced in the event.

Tommy had come in for the ride on Monksfield because he was that rare thing: a strong, senior lightweight. He never held a retainer for the ride with either the owner or trainer but, having progressed to ride the horse under bigger weights, and then by winning the Champion Hurdle itself, he naturally considered the horse 'his' ride.

Tommy had held a riding licence for nearly a quarter of a century and had suffered crippling falls, but that was the first time in his life he felt like giving up. He remembers, 'I was absolutely disgusted, and I still believe I was entitled to the ride. To say I was bitter and sore – and still am – is true, and I still don't understand why it happened.' Tommy insists that, in spite of reports to the contrary, he never fell out with either

Des McDonogh or Dessie Hughes.

Once home, Tommy's first reaction was to get rid of all the pictures of Monksfield. But he relented: 'After all, it wasn't the horse's fault, and he had given me the greatest moments of my racing life.'

Dessie Hughes and Tommy Kinane were good friends, but, as an up-and-coming professional who had himself struggled to make his name, Dessie could not allow sentimentality to get in the way: 'When it happened, Tommy was very peeved, and I don't blame him. He did not speak to me in the weighing room even though we sat next to each other. But it was just a face he was putting on in front of other people. Basically he knew it was not my fault, and down at the start of a race he was as friendly as ever.'*

Thirty years later Tommy is still upset by it. 'The biggest low of my racing life was being jocked off Monksfield. I didn't do anything wrong and was fierce disappointed. There had been a telephone strike for five months in Ireland, and that could have had something to do with it.' Today, with mobile phones, email, BlackBerries and other means of instant communication, it is easy to forget that only three decades ago to make a call from Holy Cross in Tipperary Tommy would have had to twist the handle to get through to the operator, and she would then try and connect him to the desired number – so long as there wasn't a strike on.

* Powell, *Monksfield*, p. 180.

Tommy was to gain a bittersweet revenge at Cheltenham shortly before the Champion Hurdle. Des McDonogh had entered Stranfield for the Supreme Novices Hurdle, and he booked Tommy. Dessie Hughes was also in the race, riding a horse called Killamonan. One has only to recall Tommy's kicking of his schoolteacher when he considered she had been unfair to his brother to remember that he has a temper. By his own admission, he rode Stranfield in a temper that day, like a man possessed, inspired. There was only going to be one conclusion: to win, to show that he could ride as well as the next man, if not better. As he passed the post first on the 16–1 winner he put his fist up in the general direction of Monksfield's owner in the stands.

'I never spoke to him again,' Tommy says. 'Dr Mangan was reared a long way from owning a Champion Hurdler to jock off the rider who won it for him. Nevertheless, I believe it was engineered by someone else.' He doesn't mean either Des McDonogh or Dessie Hughes. As he rode in to a reception that he remembers as even bigger than when he won the Champion Hurdle, his vocal cords let it be known in no uncertain manner that he was no back number, yelling loudly that he was not finished as a jockey yet, and 'they can't keep a good man down.'

A few races later, Tommy remained in the weighing room while his friend Dessie went out to ride an equally inspired race on Monksfield to beat Sea Pigeon and to claim the Champion Hurdle crown.

Monksfield was a once-in-a-lifetime horse. The little star

with the big heart came at the twilight of Tommy's career, but this is the horse that people remember him for. Both were fearless, with an innate will to win, the courage to throw their hearts over the obstacle and the competitive spirit that can mark the difference between victory and defeat. 'Monksfield made me, though the memories were soured a little, but he was a great bit of stuff – sharp, but he had no coltish ways in a race,' Tommy remembers. Monksfield ran another two seasons with a number of different jockeys – notably Dessie Hughes in the Champion Hurdle of 1980 in which they finished second to Sea Pigeon. That made Monksfield's Champion record two wins and two seconds.

While Monksfield was the best horse he ever rode, Tommy believes the best four-year-old he ever sat on was Monaco Prince, and that, had he not broken down, he too would have won a Champion Hurdle.

Interestingly, Tommy Kinane rode Monksfield one more time, in his last-ever race, the Royal Doulton Handicap Hurdle at Haydock in May 1980. 'I don't know how I got the ride back,' muses Tommy. It was not to have the fairytale ending. Once more set to carry 12 stone, only one other runner, Connaught Ranger on 11 stone 6 pounds, had more than 10 stone 11 pounds. It was early May, and Monksfield's coat was shining in spite of yet another long season. He thrived on racing and loved the springtime, and he went off second favourite. Turning into the straight in a handy enough position, the little horse was hampered badly and was unable to recover, finishing unplaced.

Tommy unsaddled, gave his old pal one final pat on the neck, and they went their separate ways. For Monksfield, unlike most National Hunt horses, who are geldings, it was off to a life at stud where he sired a number of winners. For Tommy, it was only another seven months until, on 29 December 1980, he too was persuaded by his family to hang up his racing boots to concentrate solely on training.

6

A splinter off the old block

Thomas (b. 1957)

I t was a sunny day on 8 July 1957, with Tommy Kinane 150 feet up a scaffold in London, when news came that his first child, a son, Thomas, had been born. About three months later, the family moved permanently back to Ireland.

Thomas's own first memory as a child is of a black motorbike skidding under a railway bridge in Clonmel and of his father Tommy, the disgusted rider, dumping it where it lay. The incident happened when Thomas was barely a year old, yet he swears he remembers it. He also recalls the horses in Powerstown Park and the fact that he wasn't allowed to go to school there because he wasn't old enough. That changed when the family moved to Holy Cross in 1962 when Thomas was nearly five and the school was happy to take him.

Soon he was riding too. Thomas reckons he started sitting up on thoroughbreds from the age of six. Before that there were two little Shetland ponies, one a sweet-natured skewbald and the other, in Thomas's words, 'a little black whore'. It would 'cart' him round the corner, heading for home, only to be confronted by Tommy, waiting with a long tom (hunting whip and thong), ready to make him turn back.

He progressed to the farm pony, Rocky, but by the time he was nine years old, Thomas was riding work on the racehorses. He vividly remembers riding a staying chaser, who would have been on the slow side, alongside his father on a faster miler. They were on the Castle Fogarty estate with big old trees dotted around the large field which was a mile and a quarter round. 'I was kicking mine on to try and keep up with Dad. Mentally, I was already trying to be a jockey.'

In 1969, when Thomas was eleven years old, the family moved to Crohane. It was here that the four young brothers really started their riding careers, although at this time Paul was only about two years old, and so his time came later.

Thomas was also keen on other sports, including boxing, a love handed down to him from his father. Thomas boxed for the county from the age of eleven to sixteen, at weights ranging from six to nine stone. He was twice beaten in the All Ireland semi-final, though he disputes one of those verdicts, if not both. 'The first time I twice knocked my opponent down, and he hardly touched me, yet he was given a unanimous verdict. I thought I'd won the next year, too, but wasn't given it.' At least with racing it's a clear-cut case of 'The first past the post is the winner.'

Thomas enjoyed running even more than boxing. Again, he represented Tipperary, and in one particular race he knew that the first twelve Tipp runners home would be eligible to run for Munster. He saved his energy enough to ensure that he finished twelfth – he was learning race craft early. He and his teammates duly arrived at the venue for the Munster race but sadly, before the race, their secretary, standing on top of the hill ready to watch the lads, collapsed and died. The team was withdrawn so they went straight to the All Ireland minus their middle, preparatory run. Here, Thomas finished sixth of the twelve Tipperary runners and eighty-fifth overall of 235 starters.

Tommy was combining race riding with training at the time, and he, too, used to go running. It could be a tough life for the lads as Tommy tried to cope with his dual role. 'He was strict and rigid, and, when he was under pressure, he could be short-tempered.' Thomas adds, 'But when he was in a good humour we'd get on his back pretending to ride him and he would "buck" us off.'

There was a time when, in a heatwave, Tommy had gone off running round the hayfield, trying to get down to 8 stone 12 pounds for a ride in Tramore. Thomas and Mick often joined him, running in decreasing circles in an effort to keep up with him, but, on this occasion, when they got to the field, they couldn't find him. Thomas says, 'It was scorching, and in the end we found him cooling off in the ditch under a hedge.'

Thomas, meanwhile, was doing well at school. It was an environment in which he thrived, and had he not been so immersed in a racing family he could easily have become an academic. It nearly happened. He loved and was good at maths, but in order to progress he needed to be in a different school, in Fethard. He moved there but either felt out of place, missed his friends or both. Whatever, he returned to his original school in Ballingarry. This meant that when he went to college in Waterford to study accountancy he had not learnt the basics that everyone else had. It meant double work, but he was progressing well and looked more than likely to make the grade.

Racing intervened. Thomas started his accountancy course in Waterford College just as he got off to a flying start in his racing career. By June he had ridden twelve winners and looked a good bet to win the Amateur Riders' title. He was also extremely popular with his college mates who enjoyed a flutter.

On 5 June in Tramore (barely ten minutes away from his college), Thomas took a crashing fall from Ribiress. He crushed three vertebrae and lost three teeth and occupied the same bed in hospital that had just been vacated by his father Tommy. He spent his nineteenth birthday on his back. (In 2009 he lost three more teeth after he was kicked on the cheek by a yearling.)

A man of iron made in the mould of his father, Thomas was back in the racing saddle three months later to ride in the Galway September meeting. It was a three-horse race, and the night before Thomas stayed in a friend's house along with his two rivals, Des McDonogh and Nicky Dee. Nicky was a top amateur, and Des was to become better known as a trainer, notably with Monksfield.

Three-runner races are notoriously tricky to ride. Nicky and Thomas let Des go off in the lead, then, just as Thomas was ready to swoop, Nicky called over to Des to go to the rail. As he did, Nicky swooped by on the outside, Thomas was stuck on the rail behind Des, and Nicky was gone beyond recall. Gamesmanship! But at least Thomas was back, and from then until the end of the season he won another six times, leaving him third overall in the amateur table with eighteen wins. It was a dream start to his career, and so, naturally, as he gained experience, his record could be expected to improve. Surprisingly, that turned out to be his best-ever season; however, he never rode fewer than twelve winners in a season.

Weight was always going to be a problem for Thomas: quite thickset and stocky, like his father Tommy and uncle Christy, he was unlike his two lean and slight brothers Jayo and Paul. Mick, as we shall see, was able to maintain a flat-racing weight once he had found the key with the help of a nutritionist.

Thomas was also a good point-to-point rider, but by 1979 he was doing well enough on the track to turn professional, just as his father's career was finally coming to an end. Thomas tried to engineer Tommy going out on a winner. Tommy had had a fall off a mare called Dunsford Lass in Punchestown, and Thomas was due to ride her in Limerick. At that stage, both Thomas and

Mick were riding at the same time as their father. Dunsford Lass was a headstrong mare, a fighter, but if her head was left alone she was good enough. The race she was entered for in Limerick was meant to be a 'steering' job, and Thomas offered to relinquish the ride in favour of Tommy so that his father could bow out on a winner – but Tommy wouldn't hear of it.

As a professional, Thomas rode mainly for his father but also for Tom Kidd and for Christy, for whom he rode more winners than anyone else. There were only two meetings a week and even fewer in the summer. The champion jockey was Frank Berry, but second to him in terms of strike rate (although not in number of wins) was Thomas, whose win rate was 21 per cent of about 150 rides; Frank's was 23 per cent from two or three times as many rides.

Thomas, always a horseman, was a 'journeyman jockey' who didn't have the high-class ammunition of better-placed jockeys, but if he was on a horse capable of winning then he was almost certain to score. Equally, he was riding in the days before the Celtic Tiger when, if he won on a promising young horse it was then likely to be sold on. One such was Chinrullah, on whom he had one ride and one win, in his great college year. He received a phone call from someone asking if he would be worth £14,500 to buy. 'He's worth double,' the young Thomas advised – and was fully vindicated when the horse went on to win the Arkle Chase at the Cheltenham Festival and a number of other high-class races.

Chinrullah came along early in Thomas's career, but he

remained the best horse he ever rode. Other good ones in his career were Smoke Charger and Multiple, on whom Thomas once beat his father on Monksfield. He also won two races at one Liverpool meeting, on Raleighstown and Multiple.

Thomas never experienced the thrill of riding over the big Aintree fences though he wanted to ride in the Topham Chase. The owner wanted to run the particular horse in the Grand National but he missed the cut, and it was by that time too late to enter for the Topham (a feature race at Aintree run over the big fences, but over a shorter distance than the Grand National). He missed out on another Topham ride, too. There was a horse called Sirrah Jay that had won a point-to-point, but, when given the ride in a 3-mile novice chase in Tipperary, Thomas told the connections he 'wouldn't get 3 miles in a horsebox' in spite of all point-to-points being 3 miles. He persuaded them instead to run him on good ground over 2 or 2½ miles, and, when conditions were right, he duly hacked up in Cork. He told them he would win a Topham. A couple of years later, having duly moved to England, he did so.

In April 1976, Thomas rode Multiple, 10 stone, in a 2-mile handicap hurdle at the Punchestown Festival for Christy. Tommy was favourite on Monksfield, carrying 11 stone 7 pounds. Thomas jumped off last of the ten and kept his horse covered up. He challenged at the last flight of hurdles where Multiple made a mistake, but he just got up to beat Frank Berry on Rostan by a head, with his father and Monksfield three lengths further back.

Thomas remembers his uncle Christy with fondness. 'He

could train,' he says, 'and I rode many winners for him.' One was on Some Story for owner Paddy Meehan, in Tralee.

He also remembers riding in Liverpool, straight after his win in Tralee. It was in 1977, and Thomas travelled in a six-seater plane from Shannon to Speke, Liverpool. He was riding Multiple on 9 stone 11 pounds. The horse's price was 50–1. Thomas had the horse in a perfect position, biding his time until making up ground rapidly. He went from last to first, hitting the front landing over the last flight in apparent perfect timing. He sprinted clear on the inside rail when, with only 20 yards to go . . . *whoosh!* A horse swept by him as if he was standing still. The rider was Jonjo O'Neill, and the horse the immortal Sea Pigeon, carrying a massive 12 stone 9 pounds.

Two days later, Multiple turned out again, and this time he was favourite for the eighteen-runner amateur riders' hurdle race that traditionally follows the Grand National (memorably won that year by Red Rum for the record-breaking third time). Thomas rode a perfect race on Multiple, and, although now carrying 10 stone 5 pounds, the pair forged clear on the run-in.

Some of Thomas's other successes for his uncle came on Raleighstown, and one of those at Liverpool has special memories for him: he won by eleven lengths, broke the course record and lost his riding claim. But it was more than that. Bob Champion was riding the favourite and leading. As he was giving his horse a breather and, doubtless, trying to dictate and slow down the pace at the same time, Thomas loomed up alongside him.

'Take your time, young fella, there's a long way to go,' Bob called across.

'Bob, you ride your fucker and I'll ride mine,' rejoined Thomas before kicking clear to win.

Afterwards, Bob congratulated the now fully fledged senior jockey. 'Well done, you knew your horse.'

Thomas and Ted Walsh both had two wins on Raleighstown. One of those for Thomas was at Liverpool when Ted was suspended – probably for a minor infringement of the Rules of Racing.

On another occasion Thomas was injured at home when a horse called Wrong Wheel reared up on him. He was forced to keep his leg up on a chair for four days just as the Galway Festival, and a fancied ride on Cherryfield on the Thursday, were looming. He decided to ride on the Wednesday 'for a run' to make sure he would be fit for the next day. He took painkillers and felt fine in the parade ring. The horse was Georgian Bay, owned, like Multiple, by Dom McParland and trained by Christy Kinane. 'I had to drive him hard for the first 1½ miles, got to the front and won, but my head was spinning. After weighing in I just grabbed my coat and disappeared into the crowds to be on my own.'

Thomas was a good professional jockey with a 'brain', but, like many other promising jump jockeys, he was plagued by injury. The back injury from Tramore came early in his career, but he also broke his shoulder in one fall and, a few years later, a foot in another. His most serious fall came in Thurles in 1988. It was a case of 'like father, like son'. The horse, Young Balladeer, owned by singer Paddy Reilly, Peter Kingston and Thomas himself, had been bought by them for £2,000 from Paddy Prendergast Junior. Heading to the last, all Thomas needed to win was a good final jump. He rode at it fearlessly, in the mould of his father, but the horse fell, and Thomas was cannoned into the ground head first. He was lucky not to end up paralysed and was warned by his doctor that another serious fall could see him in a wheelchair.

Thomas didn't give up entirely and rode some more good winners over the next ten years, but the accident spelled the end of his serious career.

Luckily, that fall coincided with a new opportunity for him when his brother Mick bought Clunemore Lodge on the Curragh, built an equine swimming pool and needed someone to manage the burgeoning business. Who better than Thomas, with a good head for business and the close family tie?

Thomas had his own family by then, having married Brigid in June 1982 in a double wedding with Mick and his bride Catherine. The way Thomas met and courted Brigid was almost a carbon copy of his parents' romance. 'We met at a dance in Thurles but she refused to dance with me,' Thomas recalls, 'but the next time she agreed, and we stayed together from there. I went home and told my mum I'd met the girl I was going to marry.'

That was in 1979, when Thomas was twenty-two. Mick and Catherine were going out at the same time and also planned to marry. Members of the family would already be coming from many parts of the world, so it seemed logical to hold a double wedding, fittingly near Cashel.

'It was brilliant,' their middle sister Kathryn remembers. 'There were 200 people. I'd come home for the weekend from Belgium and stayed for two months.' Their wedding day, 25 June 1982, was also the day, cousin Brendan remembers, that Northern Ireland beat Spain in a World Cup qualifier, thanks to the kick of Gerry Armstrong. Thomas remembers that Assert won the Irish Derby the next day for David O'Brien, the horse who had not taken on Golden Fleece, trained by David's father Vincent, at Epsom. Thomas's new brother-in-law, Eugene O'Donnell, an old friend, was travelling head lad to David O'Brien.

Today, Thomas and Brigid's daughter Brid works in Belgium, and their son Thomas (Toss) currently helps on Mick's farm.

Thomas's last two wins came on Pegus First, owned and trained by Patrick O'Leary. The first was in a maiden hurdle at Mallow, County Cork, on 1 May 1999, followed up a week later in a novice hurdle at Fairyhouse. In both rides Thomas displayed his trademark tactical skill. His last mount in the autumn of that year unseated him in Tralee. 'When the renewal form for my licence dropped through the letterbox in December I didn't even open it – I tore it in half and threw it in the bin.'

No fanfare, just a quiet exit. That was Thomas's way.

Today, Thomas lives in the bungalow at the head of the long, winding back drive to Mick's place near Naas. Thomas hunts occasionally, usually with the Tara Harriers in County Meath, where he can relax and enjoy the company of friends. His horsemanship will see him jumping the widest ditches to be found anywhere, seemingly effortlessly, as he keeps up with George Briscoe's hounds. George, in his eighties, is reluctantly no longer on a horse, but he remains held in the highest respect countywide.

Thomas works as hard as ever (an ingrained part of the Kinane family ethos), mostly driving a horsebox for an equine transport company, frequently travelling to the UK, France and beyond. Most days will find him in Mick's yard, mucking out, sweeping and looking the image of his father, bar the cigar that is part of Thomas's stable routine. He only occasionally goes racing, one of the reasons being that the time he retired coincided with former jockeys no longer being offered a free racecourse pass for life. Thomas feels that for everything such men have given to racing, and the risks and the injuries they have taken, that is the least they should be given.

One of the animals he brings in for its evening feed in the spring of 2010 is an overgrown three-year-old by Azamour, owned by Mick. He is bred for high things and is a wonderful mover but has a head that looks more like a hunter. Thomas shows me a filly that he owns himself, and his eyes light up. She is beginning to give him a good 'feel' in work. The ever-present racing hope of finding a 'good un' never fades.

7

Off to a flying start

Mick (b. 1959)

'You're not going back to school.' No ifs or buts. That was it. Mick was fifteen years old and fully expecting to return for the summer term to finish his formal education. But his father Tommy had other ideas. What had begun as a holiday job was to become permanent because owners were already asking for the sandy-haired boy to ride their horses.

When they were young teenagers, Thomas and Mick began riding out for trainer Edward O'Grady in school holidays and at weekends, and on weekdays they would ride out for their father before school. Tommy arranged for Mick to spend one

Christmas holidays (December 1974–January 1975) with Larry Greene, a vet and one of the trainers he rode for in County Tipperary. A couple of months later, Larry told Tommy he would like Mick to ride a horse called Muscari in a particular apprentices' race at Leopardstown. This meant, first, that the lad had to be apprenticed to a licensed trainer. Tommy had already arranged for him to be apprenticed to Liam Browne on the Curragh that summer, after Mick was due to leave school, and so, for the sake of the ride, the apprenticeship papers were signed earlier than originally planned.

The horse Mick rode was the hard-pulling Muscari that Tommy had himself ridden in a few races. Not long before, the lad had landed the Munster Boxing Junior Championships in the 6 stone 7 pounds division. A more surprising success was to follow, for Muscari's starting price was 16–1. Lucky Leopardstown applies to the Kinanes as Tommy, Mick and Paul all rode their first winners there, and for Mick this was on his racecourse debut. In the race, the headstrong Muscari eventually pulled his way to the front for Mick and stayed there to romp in. Michael J. Kinane had begun his racing career the way he was to go on. A number of newspaper correspondents predicted a bright future for him.

Mick went to school the next day as usual, for the end of term, little knowing it would be his last day as a schoolboy, and went up to Liam Browne's for the Easter holidays. Liam Browne, himself a former champion apprentice, earned a reputation for turning out successful budding jockeys. Mick still expected to be back with the nuns teaching him in Killenaule for one last term but instead he remained at Liam's, a tutor much tougher than the nuns and a strict military-style disciplinarian. Any rough edges there might have been would soon be knocked off, and any answering back was out of the question.

Members of his family believe it was during this period that what was to become Mick's trademark quietness was fuelled, accelerated later when fame and the accompanying press attention rolled his way. Mick could still fight his corner, but the happy-go-lucky lad, up for the craic, turned into a solemn, serious young man who said very little, in public at least. Although he could laugh and joke with his family, they more than any saw the change as it evolved over the years.

Mick had seen the difficulties his father had had with the scales for jumping – admittedly only for the lowest weights and for the occasional flat race. He was built along similar lines to Tommy and Thomas, short like them though slimmer, but not slight like his younger brothers Jayo and Paul. He still looked slightly cherubic, and he had only been in racing a year when he began a regime that is the lot of so many jockeys: eat less, sweat, take diuretics (pee pills) and laxatives. It wasn't doing much good: he was constantly hungry and tired. Eventually he saw a dietician who put him onto sensible steamed and grilled nutritious food and extra exercise. Once into the routine he was able to keep his weight down. He still expected to become a jump jockey, but Tommy persuaded him to stick at the flat, at least until his five-year apprenticeship had expired.

There is good luck, bad luck and the sort of luck you make through sheer hard work – that was Mick's category. Instead of going off with the lads during their precious evening time off, Mick would be studying films of his rides, spotting where he had gone wrong, determining to rectify mistakes the next time. Even as a fully fledged stable jockey and budding champion for Dermot Weld, for whom he worked for fifteen years from 1984, it was the same – slightly reluctantly at first, perhaps, but soon appreciating the benefit of Weld's wise words.

Later still, when he had his first Epsom Derby and a number of riding championships behind him, it was the same before the Melbourne Cup. Mick could not get to Australia more than one day ahead of the great race because he was not prepared to let down people over rides he was already committed to in Hong Kong. He knew from all accounts that the experience at Flemington racetrack, on the outskirts of Melbourne, was going to be unlike any other. And so he watched countless videotapes of the race, covering twenty years, and he also quizzed Australian jockeys in Hong Kong about it.

Time spent in reconnaissance is seldom wasted. Three years after his chosen career began, Mick was Champion Apprentice, and four years later, in 1982, by that time riding principally for Michael Kauntze, he won his first Classic. This was the Irish 2,000 Guineas on home turf at the Curragh on a horse called Dara Monarch. Appropriately, the 20–1 chance was trained by Liam Browne, Mick's first boss. Mick took up the running a furlong from home and scored by three lengths, the first Kinane to win a Classic. He was twenty-two years old.

The year 1982 was also momentous for Mick as in June, the month of his twenty-third birthday, he married Catherine, the girl who was his rock in life and who would become mother of their two daughters, Sinead and Aisling. It became almost a tradition that a Kinane did not marry a racing girl, and Catherine was no exception. Her father worked on a farm in Ballymore Eustace, County Kildare, and Mick first spotted her at a local soccer match. Mick employed a little detective work and discovered that the good-looking girl might be at a nearby dance later on. But, like others in the family, Mick's advances were spurned at first when he plucked up courage to ask Catherine to dance. Then, once they began going out together and she saw the injuries that could be piled up, even by a flat jockey, she may have wavered. In fact, the day after their wedding (there was no time for a honeymoon), Irish Derby Day at the Curragh, Mick had a fall that crushed a vertebra. And then, less than three weeks later, he was brought down again, this time in Killarney, and he broke his wrist. Probably his worst racing fall was in Hong Kong fourteen years later, when many injuries and multiple bruising included several broken ribs. But he is not his father's son for nothing, and it didn't take him too long to bounce back.

By the time of his marriage in 1982, all thoughts of winning the Grand National had given way to Derby dreams. It was not plain sailing: for one thing, he still had to waste hard, and, for another, there were some people who felt he might have a temperament problem – notably Dermot Weld, who mulled long and hard over whether or not to take him on when the position of stable jockey became vacant. He was afraid Mick might be too young and could get cocky. It was also known that in an argument he was well capable of putting his boxing prowess into practice.

Mick was now yearning for his big break: a top stable that could give him sufficient backing to bring dreams to fruition: senior championships, more and greater classics, winners around the world. All this was to happen, but not until Dermot Weld had grilled him sufficiently and then left him waiting for a month for the answer. It was 'yes'. This was in the autumn of 1983, and Mick would start the new job with the start of the 1984 flat season. But, although attached to the stable, he would not be riding its runners abroad – yet. His new boss wanted him to gain more experience and also did not want to run the risk of the young man becoming big-headed.

The newly married Dermot Weld had taken over Rosewell House Stables, on the edge of the Curragh, from his father in 1972 at the age of twenty-three. He immediately stamped his indelible mark on the Irish racing scene and further afield. He trained an amazing eighty winners from forty-five horses in his first season, and since then he has not only been Domestic Champion many times – and has made the Galway Festival his own – but he has also conquered the world. It started out as a simple business project, finding the right races for horses, often with half an eye on selling them. To begin with, this meant sending some runners to America. It culminated by winning two of the world's most prestigious flat races. Mick Kinane teamed up with them both, as we shall see. By the time Mick began working for his new boss, Dermot Weld had been at or near the top of the Irish training tree for more than a decade. Weld was a hard taskmaster, but Mick was well used to that from his father as a child and from Liam Browne as an apprentice.

In those days, the flat jockeys often spent their winters in India or Hong Kong, or both, before the advent of what is now the traditional winter in Dubai. With the exciting prospect of his new job, Mick did not hang about out there, and, as soon as he could, he presented himself to Rosewell House. By the end of that first season Mick had achieved his ambition of becoming Champion Jockey on the flat. At the end of the second, he had done so with an Irish record of 105 winners. This was four more than the previous record. Slowly but surely he also began riding some winners abroad for Dermot – in Italy and France to begin with, with the 'bigger' racing countries to follow.

Mick was doubtless anxious to progress more quickly, but he was already Domestic Champion, and Dermot Weld was shrewd in his handling of the young man. He ensured that the youthful star's confidence did not turn into conceit. Weld worked at him, honed him and almost imperceptibly prepared him for what lay ahead. It paid off, in spades. The countries that Mick won in read like a gazetteer: India, Canada and Saudi Arabia; in the better-known world centres such as Hong Kong, Japan and the United Arab Emirates; in America and Australia; and, closer to home, in Germany, Italy and France, even Austria, Spain, Slovakia and Switzerland and, of course, in the UK, where he rode numerous Classic winners: the 2,000 Guineas four times, the Derby three times, the Oaks twice and the St Leger once. He won numerous Irish Classics, and he has also won three Breeders' Cup races in the USA.

Mick was part of a ground-breaking foray to the USA in 1990, where Dermot Weld had a runner in a leg of the American Triple Crown with Go and Go in the Preakness Stakes. It was not simply a bold move, it was, in true Weld fashion, well thought through. Weld had run the colt in America as a two-year-old, ridden by an American jockey. Heavy rain meant the race was switched from turf to dirt, a surface Go and Go had never encountered before. It proved a blessing in disguise, as, by winning, he proved himself equally adept on that ground. Mick flew out a fortnight later to partner him in the Breeders' Cup Juvenile, but they were unplaced. (America was not to prove Mick's best stomping ground over the years.)

The next year, when the colt didn't show good enough form to be considered for the Epsom Derby, he was entered for the Preakness Stakes, sandwiched between the Kentucky Derby and the Belmont Stakes in the American Classic calendar. It turned into a 'steering job' for Mick Kinane, and the pair were greeted enthusiastically by the American racegoers. Dermot Weld had made history.

Even that feat was surpassed three years later when Dermot managed to get Vintage Crop through all the quarantine and other regulations for a crack at the Melbourne Cup. Although this famous race is an all-aged handicap and therefore does not bear the kudos of a Classic, it would be unwise to suggest that to an Australian. It is the day, the first Tuesday of November, on which the whole of Australia literally comes to a standstill, and Melbourne itself is like a ghost town with shops closed and inhabitants either at Flemington or gathered around television screens.

Where only a handful of Europeans had taken on the Americans on their home ground before Go and Go's success, none before had ventured to Australia. It had originally been hoped that Vintage Crop would win the Champion Hurdle at Cheltenham for his owner Michael Smurfit, whose company sponsored the race for many years, but eventually he proved better at long-distance flat races, notably the Irish St Leger, which he won twice. It was after the first of these, in 1993, that he travelled on to Australia for the first time.

It was also the first time Mick Kinane had ever been Down Under, and he was riding on a high.

The Irish St Leger was one thing, but earlier in the year he had won the Epsom Derby for the first time, riding the second string, Commander in Chief, for Newmarket trainer Henry Cecil, whose Tenby was odds-on to win. Commander in Chief, by Dancing Brave, slaughtered the high-class field. In typical fashion, instead of staying for the celebrations, bar tea with the Queen in the Royal Box, Mick was back riding at the Curragh that very evening. Like his father at Cheltenham fifteen years before, he organised a couple of crates of champagne for the jockeys' room, then sped to the airport. He arrived in time for one ride near the end of the card. The horse he rode was 4–1 on, and he looked like hacking up when an unconsidered horse passed him. The sport is truly a great leveller. But that night, at the impromptu party Catherine had organised at Clunemore Lodge, less than a mile away from the Curragh racecourse, all the talk revolved around Mick's epic Derby.

Mick cut it nearly as fine in getting to Melbourne, but he had done his homework assiduously, and it paid off. Not everything went their way in the race, but Vintage Crop kept doing more every time he was asked, and in the end he won the 2-mile marathon going away. Although winning the Melbourne Cup was momentous, it was not until he had passed the post that Mick realised just how much the race meant to the Australians – he was literally fêted and lauded from all directions, and, as for media, he could barely imagine how many there were. It was one of the most riotous receptions he had ever ridden into.

Back home in Crohane, County Tipperary, Tommy and Frances were asleep when the phone woke them at 4 a.m. It was Ned, telling them the momentous news. Of all his second son's notable feats, this is the one Tommy Kinane remembers with the greatest pride.

Michael Smurfit was unable to attend Vintage Crop's historic Melbourne Cup win, nor the following year (when that same Australian press was highly critical of Mick's riding), but he was present two years later when in defeat he believes Vintage Crop ran one of his best races for (as he told the author), 'the incomparable Dermot Weld and the dynamic Mick Kinane.'

During the early to mid-1990s, Mick turned his occasional winter visits to Hong Kong into permanent six-month stays, riding for ex-pat David Oughton, originally from Sussex. He bought a flat, rode work early in the mornings, raced the two days a week and, during the rest of the time, became much more relaxed than he could at home, able to spend more time with Catherine and on the golf course and so on. Tommy and Frances became regular visitors and loved the atmosphere, which was unlike any other they had ever encountered before.

Mick had liked Hong Kong from his first visits in the late 1980s, and Dermot Weld first sent a runner there in 1990, unplaced, but a year later Mick won the Invitation Bowl at Sha Tin riding Dermot Weld's Additional Risk. Once again Dermot was being a pioneer among trainers, this being the first European-trained horse to win in Hong Kong. Mick twice rode the winner of the Hong Kong Derby, on Sound Print in 1992 for P. C. Kan and on Che Sara Sara in 1996 for David Oughton. Among the winners he rode during his sojourns there were the 1993 Invitation Bowl on Winning Partner, hot on the heels of his ground-breaking Melbourne Cup victory, and two Queen Elizabeth II cups on Deerfield in 1994 and on Red Bishop a year later.

Hong Kong, with its warm climate and limited amount of racing, was something of a busman's holiday for Mick. It kept his eye in and retained his peak fitness for the number-one position at Weld's, back home in Ireland, where he continued to regularly top the leading rider's table.

Mick remained with Dermot Weld for fifteen fruitful years. Offers came and went during that time, including from the United Arab Emirates's Sheikh Mohammed. This promised to be the world's top job for a jockey, but Mick preferred to stay in Ireland. A year later, a compromise deal was struck with the Sheikh which meant that Mick rode his horses in major races when not conflicting with Dermot Weld, such as Opera House in the 1993 Eclipse Stakes at Sandown and King's Theatre in the 1994 King George.

The horses he won on down through his career include the crème de la crème, spanning more than three decades: Carroll House, which won the 1989 Prix de l'Arc de Triomphe, and Montjeu, which won the same race ten years later. A third, even mightier, was to come. During his time at Rosewell House Mick rode more than 1,000 winners for Dermot Weld. He was Champion Jockey many times while there, and, by the end of his career, he had been Champion Jockey of Ireland thirteen times.

Racing stables regularly go through jockey-go-rounds akin to transfer transactions in Association Football, and both bring with them much advance speculation and press fodder. Finally, in 1999, Mick made the wrench from Weld's and joined Aidan O'Brien's stable, taking over from Christy Roche who was retiring.

8

A love of horses

Jayo (b. 1960)

'A total love affair with the racehorse' is how Tommy's third son Jayo sums up his involvement with racing. 'When I look at a thoroughbred in Ballydoyle, and I see one with quality, and I sit on it – that can't be put in words.' One could add that Jayo has a love affair with life itself, including many other interests, in addition to a successful and enduring marriage with Antoinette. Horse racing is not part of her lifestyle, and this, says Jayo, has its advantages – because 'if you've been given a bollocking by a horse's trainer, assistant trainer, trainer's wife, trainer's daughter, owner, punters, whoever, the last thing you want is to go home to a wife who is also telling you how to ride!'

After his exploits on Rocky and Goodman Friday, a life in racing became inevitable for Jayo, and he was still at school when his father apprenticed him. 'Dad was a great rider, brilliant, tough as a boot, and, from the hips up – his arms and hands – he was muscular. He taught us that unless you get into the top four or five you have to diversify into business because life as a jump jockey can end in one day. It's industrialists and businessmen who own the horses – we're just the pinheads who ride them.' But Jayo wouldn't have had it any other way.

In the summer of 1975, when Jayo was fifteen, Tommy sent him to Jim Bolger when Jim was training in Clonsilla, Dublin, before his move to Coolcullen, County Carlow. While there, Jayo also sometimes babysat for Jim and Jackie Bolger and read stories to the children, Una (now married to top Irish flat jockey Kevin Manning) and Fiona.

'Jim did his best to get me a win on my first ride' – Jayo recalls the day in 1976 'as if it was yesterday'. It was a 1½-mile apprentice race in Naas, and Jayo was set to ride a big strong mare called Silvine who had won over hurdles. She was to carry 10 stone 4 pounds, and Jayo weighed just 6 stones 4 pounds. He was sixteen and had only been riding a few short years. 'She pulled like a train and led until the last stride. I was beaten a short head.'

When Jayo tried to lift the saddle and lead, weighing 4 stone, off the mare in the unsaddling enclosure, an official had to help him and then put it on his lap on the weighing scales.

'I was exhausted and couldn't feel my arms or legs afterwards!' The horse who beat him was Tasseltip, ridden by Pat Murphy, now a trainer and TV race pundit.

Jayo went straight into jumping for Tommy, though he did ride a winner on the flat for Jim Bolger a few years later – on Abolitionist in Down Royal. 'He told me not to come home unless I won!'

Jayo can take pride in having nurtured youngsters and having given them a kind introduction to the stresses and strains of the racecourse so that when they were ready for it they would be taken over by a top professional. In his heart, though, he wished he had retained those rides himself.

Jayo is fulsome in his praise of his brother Mick. 'He's one in a million. It takes a lifetime to hit his level, and only one can be the best. He's some rider, probably the best we'll ever see. I grew up with people introducing me as Tommy Kinane's son and nowadays as Mick's brother. That can be a hindrance in that it takes away identity, and people want to get to know me because of him.'

He admits it was tough starting out in racing. Most of the big Irish yards had established retained jockeys: 'You couldn't get in through their gates in the 1970s and 1980s, and forty or fifty freelances would be competing for rides long before mobile phones.' Also, there were only a couple of meetings a week in Ireland, limiting opportunities further.

Nevertheless, Jayo was busy and rode out his claim before he was twenty-one, driving the length and breadth of the island, sometimes for just one ride that would barely pay his petrol. One of the contemporary jockeys to help show him the ropes early on was Paddy Kiely.

Jayo was riding for trainers such as Jim Dreaper ('the nicest of all men that ever drew breath, loyal and uncomplicated'), Robin Kidd in Northern Ireland and Willie Rock ('a man of honour'). It was Willie who started off Tony McCoy on his historic career path. The fellow Ulsterman is favourite to win the 2010 BBC Sports Personality of the Year.

Another piece of history was created the year Jayo rode Braes O'Tully in the 1984 Irish Grand National, won for the first (and so far only) time by a female jockey, Ann Ferris, on Benton Boy, trained by her father Willie Rooney. For Jayo it was one of his most exhilarating rides because, in spite of 'having a jaw like a crocodile' (meaning hard-mouthed and strong), Braes O'Tully was also one of the best and fastest jumpers Jayo every rode. Furthermore, trainer Willie Rock would never send him home 'without a few pounds in his pocket'.

Another character he rode for was the cigar-smoking Billy Boyers from Sligo, who 'did more thinking than talking'. Jayo rode High Diver for him in the Irish National but was brought down by Pearlstone (ridden by Tony Mullins). 'He was fancied big time, and he was cantering at the time – I'm sure we would have won for his owner, Paul Clarke,' Jayo recalls. Flower Master was another memorable ride. Jayo won four races on him, including the Blazers Chase at Galway for owner ex-Celtic player Martin O'Neill, who is now manager of Aston Villa. 'He had a mouth like a hippo and was a very difficult ride; he would barely rise two feet at a 4 foot 6 inch fence. He was a nightmare at a fence, but I was young and brave as a lion.'

Jayo also rode for trainer Michael Scott from Moate, County Westmeath, whose parents had trained Thyestes Chase winner African Moon. For trainer Richard Lister of Gorey he was successful on Anita's Prince, who was also useful on the flat. 'I rode all his work at home, and he was like a rocket ship!' says Jayo. He also rode for Paddy Mullins – 'a gentleman and a pure and utter genius'.

Jayo learnt a lot with Tommy and won some good races for him, as well as helping on the farm, schooling youngsters and taking them hunting. One day, riding work with Tommy, Jayo realised just how competent a rider his father was. They were both on lazy horses, pushing them out, and Jayo observed how Tommy was pulling his horse together and pushing it at the same time. He also recalls how classy Tommy looked in his later career as a jockey when he rode with much shorter stirrup leathers and how he could approach a last fence 'as if it wasn't there'. It was at home, riding alongside his father, that Jayo learnt how to squeeze a horse with his heel 'so the other jockeys couldn't see how much you had in hand'.

Jayo knew how difficult it might be to make it in the jumping game. He was to find that times could be tough. 'Sometimes it is the toss of a coin. It didn't help me that I was never hard on a horse. I "minded" a lot of horses for owners, making them, and then when they were ready to win they would get a top jockey. I found that hard. I was good, but I was never barbaric, a fault I'm happy to live with – I was too much in love with horses and have no regrets.'

In 1978, Jayo received a telephone call from Martin Lynch who had been injured, asking him if he could ride Brown's Barn in the Dunboyne Chase the next day. Naturally Jayo accepted – but he still went on a prearranged night out. It was 3 a.m. when he got in, but he rode Brown's Barn in exemplary fashion for a famous victory for trainer Bob Jolley at 14–1. Jayo explains that the way he got so many rides was that he was prepared to drive to stable yards to ride work and school (practice jumping over steeplechase fences or hurdles) and to racecourses all over the country. It paid off – he missed the Claimers Championship by just one win at the age of twenty-one in 1981.

Jayo won six races on Smoke Charger, including the Connaught National in Sligo in June 1979 and a conditional chase at the National Hunt Festival at Punchestown two years later. Smoke Charger was a lovely horse that Tommy trained for owner W. Fannon, and Tommy sometimes rode him in races as well. Smoke Charger's Connaught National victory was the six-year-old's third win of the season. He came home clear in Sligo's feature event ahead of Giolla Deachar, Kilcoleman and the Jonjo O'Neill-ridden Dromard.

Smoke Charger was a character, who, for any other rider, would deign to do one lap of work at home and then pull himself up. He wouldn't stand still, being always fidgety, and he was a horse who needed patience. Jayo looked after him, and the pair built up a bond. Jayo's key to the horse at home was to ride him on a loose rein. Almost black, with a white star and 'great wise eyes', he would kick other lads who entered his stable, but Jayo could sleep with him – literally. 'If ever I fell out with Dad, which was quite frequent, I would spend the whole night sleeping curled up with him. He was very special. He started me off as a conditional jockey, and we were still together years later.'

Once Smoke Charger was taken to a racecourse he was in his element. He won thirteen races all told, on any type of ground from rock hard to bottomless bog – which is how the ground could best be described when he won the Connaught National. In May 1982, he won a chase in Gowran Park, ridden by Thomas. It was a six-runner race, and two of the other horses were ridden by Jayo and their cousin Martin.

In the summer of 1983, Smoke Charger was storming to a famous fourteenth victory and was a fence clear at the penultimate obstacle in Roscommon. Jayo was riding his pal. Four strides after the fence, the horse's leg snapped. It went off like a gunshot – a devastating blow to a devoted stable and a rotten end to an honourable horse. The downside of racing.

Jayo earned a reputation as a good jockey. One of his purple patches was between Christmas 1981 and New Year. The Sean Graham Hurdle was part of the Leopardstown Christmas Festival, and Jayo ran out a six-length winner on Mister Niall, trained by his father.

Four days later, Jayo teamed up with one of the best horses he ever rode, Rambling Buck. He has special reasons for remembering him. The gelding was trained by John Kenny from Roscrea, who 'could produce a horse in good nick', and the occasion was Punchestown on 30 December 1981. Rambling Buck started at 5–1 for the 3-mile chase. Jayo weighed out in the colours of owner John Kenny – dark blue with white speckles – and cantered down to the 3-mile start. In the distance were the Wicklow Mountains. The pair beat the favourite, Kilreelig, by ten lengths that felt like 'half a fence' to the delighted rider. It was the ride on which the twenty-one-year-old jockey rode out his claim. (Having achieved a certain number of winners meant he could no longer claim a weight allowance against senior jockeys in a race.) And it was the first time that Jayo was rewarded with a decent monetary present as a jockey, in addition to his percentage. Rambling Buck was sold to England for big money, an almost inevitable occurrence in those days. The highly respected National Hunt trainer Tim Foster won fourteen races with him.

He rode another good winner on Sedgefield in July 1986 when he had a trainer's licence for a spell. The horse was Jaytek Boy, a very highly strung animal owned by Jim Cringan and ridden by Michael 'Quiver' Moloney, in a conditional rider's race.

Another highly talented chaser that Jayo partnered was called Zendalesa, trained by Robin Kidd in County Down. The temperamental gelding had run out in his previous two starts, for two different jockeys, and so not surprisingly he started at long odds when Jayo teamed up with him in Navan in the early 1980s. Once more Zendalesa attempted to get the better of his rider, but this time he had Jayo to reckon with. The horse 'cocked its jaw' and attempted to run out to the left on the bend after the finishing post on the first circuit. Not for the first, or last, time, Jayo found the key to a difficult horse. He gave him a sharp crack down the shoulder and finished third. The pair went on to win six races: Naas, Punchestown and three or four times at Down Royal, often on top weight. Zendalesa never won for any other rider.

They travelled over to England for the Embassy Premier Chase final at Ascot on 14 January 1984, a spine-tingling occasion. Nine turned out for the prestigious event, and, although it was Zendalesa's first run of the season, Jayo hoped for a good run. Unfortunately for him, the saddle slipped at the water jump, an obstacle not used in Ireland, and because of that he was unable to move on Zendalesa – if he had, he would have landed on the deck, so all he could do was coast home. Up front the favourite Ballinacurra Lad, also from Ireland, trained by Joe Crowley, was left clear at the last. In second was the future Aintree Grand National winner West Tip. The world was at Zendalesa's feet, but that summer, at only eight years of age, he broke his leg at home and had to be put down.

Attending Goffs Sales one day in 1984, Jayo met Cumbrian trainer Gordon Richards, who already had one Grand National under his belt: Lucius in 1978. The trainer invited the young jockey to come across the water. Jayo accepted but first fulfilled his commitment to Jim Dreaper to ride Kilreelig in the Galway Plate, in July, the prestigious summer steeplechasing handicap and the highlight of the now-week-long annual racing festival. The horse was a tearaway and was ten lengths clear by the first fence and finished a not-disgraced fifth.

Jayo then he packed his bags for what promised to be his big career break. At the time, Neale Doughty was Richards' stable jockey, but with over 120 horses in the yard there should be plenty of rides. There was racing six days a week in the UK (Sunday racing came in about ten years after Ireland, which introduced it in 1985 – and Sunday point-to-points had for long been part of the Irish scene), and there were many trainers in the area who would be happy to avail of Jayo's services.

So it was to the wild, woolly and beautiful heights around Penrith, and from day one he was 'mad about Gordon'. At first he stayed with neighbours because there was no other room for him at Gordon Richards' place. Of Gordon Jayo says, 'There is no doubt that he was the best National Hunt trainer ever, and if he had lived halfway down the country he would have taken over all of England.' Richards was able to nurture great longevity in his horses, was 'gentle with a horse, and was an uncanny big man. He understood horses – and he was good to us boys.'

Jayo found he got on well with all the northern trainers. He lived in the UK from the early 1980s to the early 1990s. In those days there was a complete break in British National Hunt racing for a couple of months each summer but Ireland kept going with its mixed meetings – one of the highlights of the summer being the three-day festival in beautiful Killarney. Before Jayo returned home for the summer, Gordon Richards offered him the job of stable jockey for the following season. This was Jayo's big break.

Jayo was free of his apprenticeship to his father by this time, and the racing world lay at his feet. Only a few jockeys make it to the top, let alone the pinnacle, and so it follows that the majority do not. Most, however, love the game, never stop trying and, a bit like a fisherman, continue to dream of 'the big one'. For the jump jockeys it is even harder as not only do they need the luck of a good horse in addition to ability but also there is the ever-present danger of injury. Many an undoubted future star has been sidelined, and any injured jockey will tell you that it is that much harder to regain good rides on his return from the sidelines.

Jayo is a typical example. Supremely talented and a light-weight, his is a 'might-have-been', a 'nearly' story. He achieved his big break in being appointed as first jockey to Gordon Rich-ards in Cumbria but shortly before he was to take it up he was badly injured in Killarney.

It was in buoyant mood that Jayo drove down to Killarney to ride the odds-on favourite Star of Coole for Willie Treacy in the novice chase. They were approaching the third-last fence when the horse two away to his right suddenly veered left, knocking into the middle horse, who, in a knock-on domino effect, caused Star of Coole to crash through the wooden wing. It happened so quickly, and it was impossible to take remedial action; the horse had nowhere else to go. A piece of steel went through Jayo's leg just below the knee and out the other side – he was lucky not to lose it. The ligaments were sewn together, and Jayo began the long, slow weeks of convalescence.

Gordon Richards rang Tommy to say he had entered five horses at Market Rasen, each with a good chance, with the intention of getting Jayo off to a good start in his prestigious new job. When would he be fit to ride? Jayo was unable to answer for certain. It was to be six to eight months before he regained full strength, and so reluctantly Jayo gave up his dream job before it had begun and recommended Phil Tuck to Gordon. Phil Tuck went on to ride ninety-eight winners for the great trainer.

Once fit, Jayo returned to the north of England, where he rode for Richard Allen and Ken Oliver, landing the job of stable jockey to Ken Oliver later that year, 1985. It remains Jayo's biggest regret in his racing life that he did not return to Gordon. Gordon tried to persuade him one day when they met in Hexham but Jayo opted to stay with the Olivers.

Gordon Richards trained more than 2,000 winners, including 118 in the 1980–1 season, before his untimely death in 1998 at the age of sixty-eight. Tributes poured in from all quarters of racing and beyond. He was the first man over whose death Jayo had cried. His first top-class horse was Playlord, and, although he trained two Grand National winners – Hallo Dandy in addition to Lucius – probably his greatest moment came when the grey One Man won the 1998 Queen Mother Champion Chase (having twice previously finished sixth in the Cheltenham Gold Cup). Without doubt his saddest came a few short weeks later when the stunning grey was killed in a fall over the Mildmay (conventional birch) course at Liverpool.

Jayo plied his skill in the north of the UK, about nine years all told, including a brief spell when he trained in Scotland, continuing to return home to Ireland for the summer meetings. He also rode out for Vincent O'Brien and is quick to acknowledge how much the master of Ballydoyle taught him, mostly through observation. Jayo's uncle Billy was a work rider there for more than thirty years, which gave Jayo the precious entrée. 'Virtually the only way to get in otherwise was with a letter from the Pope!' Jayo jokes. 'There would be seventy lads queuing for a five- or six-day trial.'

One of the things Jayo noticed there was that Vincent allowed horses to work (that is, canter) downhill, something that remains rare. The majority of trainers work their horses uphill or on the level. Jayo asked the great man the reason and was told, 'to develop their speed'. Vincent explained that the 'speed' muscle in a racehorse was stretched when it went downhill, and so this was something he developed. 'Vincent didn't say twenty other words to me in three summers,' Jayo says, 'but he answered what he thought was a considered question.'

During the three summers that Jayo was with Vincent O'Brien he was riding alongside the likes of Pat Eddery, John Reid and Cash Asmussen. Vincent wanted Jayo to become a permanent part of the staff and did his best to persuade him. He offered him a house, £175 per week and a car. Newly married, in 1987, it was tempting, but the lure of the jumping game was too strong. Jayo was still hoping to scale the heights as a jockey.

It was the next year, in 1988, that he had his only ride in the Aintree Grand National. Jayo and his cousin Martin, son of his uncle Dan, both rode. Jayo's mount Polly's Pal and Martin's, Brass Change, were 100–1 outsiders, both on the bottom weight of ten stone, and both ten-year-olds. It is a day, or rather weekend, that Jayo will never forget. Like all aspiring jump jockeys he had always wanted to be there, and, more than twenty years later, he still describes the occasion as 'amazing'. As for the digs that he stayed in, he remembers that as 'some grotty B&B without a pot to pee in'.

What's more, he was never paid for the ride – no more than the mandatory minimum riding fee, that is. Traditionally, a Grand National jockey will be paid considerably more – not only for the expense of getting there and staying over for a couple of nights but also because of the prestige of the event and the increased danger. For a journeyman jockey, as Jayo freely describes himself, there are some rides that can end up costing more than the fee, especially if hundreds of miles are travelled for one ride. But a young man making his way in the game cannot afford to turn down an offered ride.

It happened to Jayo once at Cheltenham when it cost him around £400 to make the journey and the fee was modest. On the other hand, there was another time at Cheltenham when he was told he would be paid £5,000 if he could simply get a horse called Lord Muff round. 'Not a hope,' said champion amateur Enda Bolger when he heard of the deal; he had had a nasty fall from the horse in a lowly point-to-point. Nevertheless, Jayo managed the feat, and the owner duly paid up.

But back to Aintree. Nerves were not a part of Jayo's make-up, and he relished the challenge ahead. The year 1988 was the last but one that Becher's Brook was jumped 'the old way' before the landing side of the ditch was filled in. Although the fence has remained the same size, it is a safer landing for horses, and a faller now can no longer slip back into the ditch.

It was way back in 1961 that the take-off sides of the fences were given a 'skirt', making them more inviting by not being upright; nevertheless, the actual height remained the same. The minimum height for a normal steeplechase fence is 4 foot 6 inches, made of birch with a green 'apron'. At Aintree, the fences are mostly between 4 foot 10 inches and 5 foot high, made of thorn and covered in a layer of spruce, but Becher's has a 'drop' on the landing side of about 7 feet which can catch out a horse. The Chair is the biggest of all, standing at 5 foot 2 inches high with a wide ditch in front of it, and the open ditches at the third fence and Valentine's Brook are also big ones. A tricky one is the Canal Turn, where the course veers sharply left at a 45-degree angle immediately after it.

At 4½ miles, the race is the longest in the British calendar, and it also has an exceptionally long run in. There is no other course like it, making it truly unique, as it has been since its inception in 1839. Even back then it drew the crowds – and the critics. Some horses will take a natural liking to it, a few an instant loathing. Some trainers will make a replica fence at home to school an intended runner over, a practice that was begun by Irish trainers on the Curragh back in the nineteenth century. Others trust in their horse's natural aptitude.

It is every jockey's dream to win, and none will consider his horse a no-hoper, even at 100–1, and so all Jayo Kinane felt was keen anticipation. The day before the race he walked the course with Dick Francis and Ginger McCain's wife Beryl. Dick advised Jayo to stick to the inside because it was the shorter way and the horse would stay on better once the initial first mile was run, as it always was, at such a fast pace.

At last the tapes went up, and, to the roar of the crowd, Jayo kicked Polly's Pal out in the front, yet by the time they reached the first fence they were in about tenth place, so fast were the horses galloping. Jayo takes up the story: 'It all happened so quickly: the first few fences just came and went. We made our way down the inside to jump Becher's in ninth, tight to the rail. He was a small horse but very nimble, and I was thinking of Dick's advice. At the fence after Becher's a horse called Marcolo lost his rider, Venetia Williams.' (Today, Venetia is a top UK trainer with a Grand National winner, Mon Mome, under her belt.) Jayo continues, 'I jumped the Canal Turn on the inside but the loose Marcolo cannoned into us, and we were knocked over!'

That was the end of his Aintree dreams.

For Jayo's cousin Martin it was also one of life's most memorable experiences. He was riding for Peter Jones at the time and had a good ride booked for the mares' steeplechase final on the Friday. His father Dan travelled over from Ireland, and the pair drove up to Aintree on the Thursday. The first thing they had to do was find somewhere to stay – a difficult, near-impossible task so close to the big day. After a fruitless drive around they came back to the Melling Road and spotted a woman and her granddaughter about to enter her house. They wound down the window and asked if she knew where they could find a bed and breakfast. Martin probably mentioned that he was riding in the National, and the woman – he wishes he could remember her name – promptly invited them to stay with her for nothing. She refused to take a penny from them so they gave her a gift, and a couple of years later, when Martin was in the area, he went to see her again.

His ride on Silent Surrender on Friday got him off to a flying start when she won over the Mildmay (birch) course in the mare's final. Naturally it put connections in buoyant mood before the big race for all that Brass Change was a 'no-hoper'. Peter had suggested early in the year that they 'stick Brass Change in the National' for the fun of it, for a day out.

Martin recalls, 'He knew the horse wasn't good enough but he was willing to give it a go.' Martin walked the course on the Thursday and thought to himself, *This is big.* 'The first ditch, the third fence, is so big you could drive a tractor down it. I knew the horse jumped well and was clever but he was lazy and needed pushing, and 4½ miles is a long way to be pushing a horse!'

Brass Change made it as far as the twenty-seventh fence, the one after Valentine's, where he fell. In truth, Martin knew he should have pulled him up before it, but, like any Grand National jockey, if he couldn't win it his next ambition was to get round. 'We were all delighted with him, and it was a great buzz.'

Jayo did well for the trainer when winning the Tennent's Special Chase Handicap at Ayr on Aden Apollo, but one of his most exciting prospects came with Black Hawk Star. The horse won six races including the Grand National Trial at Haydock in 1986. This earned him a 25–1 quote for the Grand National, and Jayo was naturally full of hope. 'He stood 17.2 hands but moved like a ballet dancer. I hoped to win the National with him but he was injured when he was turned out in a field.'

In 1999, at the age of thirty-nine, Jayo called time on his race-riding career. He was riding a horse called Cormack Lady, trained in Sligo by Mick McElhone in Down Royal, a happy hunting ground, and the horse had a good chance of winning. But when Jayo went to pick up his whip his left shoulder dislocated, and he was beaten. It was a recurring, painful problem, and he knew the moment had come for him to retire. Perhaps he could go out on a win . . . A couple of weeks later he was to ride at the Galway Festival on what was to be his father's last runner as a trainer, and Jayo's last race over jumps. Daenis (Sinead spelt backwards) ran well, but instead of a dream ending unfortunately he broke down (strained a tendon).

A love of horses

When Jayo returned to Ireland from Scotland he was a work rider for Dermot Weld for about seven years, living near Naas. He also began a wedding-cars business when he spotted a niche in the market, and it quickly grew. It was often racing-connected brides and grooms that he drove. He started with one Rolls-Royce and ended with seven along with a number of vintage cars. Eventually Jayo sold the business as a going concern and returned to his native Tipperary where he joined the Ballydoyle team. Today, he works for Vincent O'Brien's successor there, Aidan O'Brien (unrelated). Jayo says, 'Aidan leads from the front. Mentally and physically he works harder than any other trainer.'

Jayo, Antoinette, their son Dean and their dog Shadow, daughter of Tommy's Patterdale Carrie, live between New Inn and Cashel, about two minutes away from Ballydoyle. Jayo rides out there between three and four lots every morning, and in October–November 2008 he spent twenty-eight days in Melbourne with Honolulu in his preparation for the Melbourne Cup in which, on firm ground, he finished unplaced. He is full of praise for the Australian way of doing things. 'They really promote their racing, it's a wonderful sport. The press is very keen to print their racing.'

Dean (b. 23 February 1989)

If Jayo grew up being introduced as Tommy Kinane's son, and in later life as Mick Kinane's brother, his son Dean, now twenty-one, is adamant: he has grown up being 'Jayo's son'. Jayo is well known and respected in County Tipperary in his own right. Local people went to school with him and followed his exploits on the raceourse – those people's children have been to school with Jayo's son, Dean.

Jayo and Antoinette never forced Dean into riding, and he was allowed to choose his own hobbies. In the sporting sphere he has become a talented rugby player, playing for Cashel. Liz Prendergast in Kildare taught both Antoinette and Dean to ride, and, at the age of eighteen, Dean spent a year and a half – two summers sandwiching his gap year – riding out at nearby Aidan O'Brien's. Jayo was already one of Aidan's tried-and-trusted work riders.

While Dean was at Ballydoyle, the colt Scorpion returned from Hong Kong with a fractured pelvis. It was feared he would never run again, but eventually he began walking exercise. By Montjeu, he was a fractious fellow, and it was to Dean that Aidan entrusted him for his slow road to recovery. 'He asked me to mind him, and see what happens,' Dean says. 'I learnt so much from Aidan in the way of horse husbandry, and he brought me a long way. I was riding out in the mornings and doing horses over in the evenings.' At first, when Scorpion was asked to leave the string and walk back while the rest went on to canter, he was quite fiery, but Dean just talked to him calmly.

As a three-year-old, Scorpion had finished second in the Irish Derby to the French-trained Hurricane Run and took a Classic by winning the St Leger at Doncaster. But he finished unplaced in the Arc and was off the course for a full year. When he returned in the autumn of his four-year-old year he failed to win in three attempts. It was different at five. His five runs yielded two wins and two seconds in the highest class. His effort in beating stable companion Septimus, ridden by Mick Kinane, in Epsom's 2007 Coronation Stakes, over the Derby course and distance, was ultra game, but nearly his best race of all was in defeat for his swansong in the 2007 Irish St Leger. In a brave effort to make all the running, he was only just caught by the popular Yeats. And much of the credit for that goes to a non-racing member of the Kinane clan: Dean.

The end of Dean's gap year and the start of a college course in mechanical engineering meant that Jayo had taken over Scorpion by the time of that memorable Irish St Leger. Horse and work rider were booked for a trip to Melbourne for the famous Melbourne Cup, but neither made it. Riding out at Ballydoyle one morning Jayo got a fall off a two-year-old on the gallops, and it kicked him, leaving him with a broken neck and jaw. Scorpion travelled to Australia but broke down while exercising.

Another horse that Jayo normally looked after, Mahler, finished a brave third in probably the most famous staying flat-race handicap in the world. Jayo had led up Pat Smullen – 'such a nice chap' – on Mahler in the Epsom Derby in which he finished unplaced behind Authorised.

Although Dean does not intend to make horses or racing his career – he was awarded his degree in mechanical engineering in June 2010 – he enjoyed every day of his time at Ballydoyle. When he left in 2007, the staff of the Blue Yard, which he was mostly attached to, threw a party for him and presented him with an inscribed bronze and framed photograph of him riding Song of Hiawatha leading Mahler on the gallops. 'Father and son in action together – magic,' says Jayo.

In the summer of 2010, Dean returned to Ballydoyle to work for Aidan again.

9

The one that got away?

Paul (b. 27 March 1967)

The rural Meath pub was heaving with after-hunting drinkers. They regaled each other with stories of the day's derring-do: the biggest ditch, the narrowest escape, so-and-so didn't make it. Another round is called. As with fishermen and the weight of their catch, so the size of the ditches that had been jumped during the day increase in the telling. In the background a TV is showing At the Races.

Suddenly, a cheery voice chirps up, 'That's my brother!' He looks around but not a lot of attention is given. 'My brother's won!' he tries again, and, innocently, I look towards him querying, 'Mick Kinane?!'

Paul is pleased as punch to tell me of yet another win from his brother. Out hunting that day, Paul has been 'making' a young flashy chestnut hunter. He puts it at a place – a high hedge – that surely no one else will attempt. The horse thinks about it momentarily then responds to Paul's urging. They soar over while everyone else goes round a different way, either smaller or through a gate. It was a place that would be big for a seasoned hunter, let alone a novice.

Tommy Kinane states that, as a lad, Paul was more of a natural horseman than Mick. His brothers confirm it. Becoming famous or not in racing is often a case of time, place, circumstances – the 'what ifs' of life – and, in Paul's case, character. As a fourteen-year-old he rode in pony races, a circuit that has seen so many talented Irish jockeys emerge, many of them becoming top professional riders, such as Norman Williamson, Charlie Swan, Adrian Maguire, Barry Geraghty, Jamie Spencer and Paddy Flood, plus the outstanding female amateur Nina Carberry. Pony races (a misnomer, as a number of races on each card are for horses) can be fairly hairy affairs, run either on a beach or in a tight circuit round the perimeter of a field that is often only approximately a half-mile circuit. This can lead to some frenzied, cutthroat tactics with courageous young jockeys getting plenty of practice on bends, straights, passing other horses, seeing a gap, closing a gap. There will be ponies bucking, rearing, running away, refusing to start, slipping up on the tight bends, unseating their young jockeys. The bolder lads will do their best to intimidate the starter to try and get a flying start,

The one that got away?   133

and at the end whips will be flying.

It is the sort of environment in which the young Paul thrived, and he could hold his own and more with any of them. If the Kinanes had a reputation for being fearless then Paul could sometimes border on a foolhardiness that was slow to leave him. A plus part of that was confidence and enthusiasm which he could be certain to transmit to his mounts, enabling them to win races that with a less confident rider they might not. But the downside was that his brand of confidence could all too easily be interpreted as cockiness, and that didn't always go down well with the powers that be.

It is no surprise that the young Paul became one of the most stylish hurdle-race riders to grace the Irish scene as a teenager. Tall but neat in the saddle, he had no weight problems for jumping because he was, and remains, 'stick' thin. But it meant that doing the weight for the flat was harder because there was simply no more weight to come off.

At the age of seventeen he won on his first visit to Leopardstown, riding Champagne Brigade in a hurdle race, trained by his father. Only one year later, at eighteen, Paul was leading claiming rider of Ireland. The world was his oyster. A spell with Monica Dickinson in Yorkshire was probably doomed to personality conflict, but travelling to Japan, Australia and New Zealand, where he was one of the leading jockeys over jumps, gave him a valuable glimpse of the sport internationally.

In Ireland, Paul rode many winners for his uncle Christy, and he also won a good four-year-old hurdle race at Punchestown on Clusheen for trainer Joe Crowley in December 1985. 'I had a great time riding but I prefer to put it behind me now,' Paul says. 'I enjoyed it while it happened.'

Hunting remains Paul's great passion, and he has combined that with business for a number of years by buying, making and selling quality hunters. That meant, of course, that his love of hunting also became his livelihood, hunting locally with the Kildares and the Taras as well as further afield, down south and, more recently, in the north, with the South Tyrone – 'the best pack in Ireland!' Paul declares. Preparation at home is the key to making a hunter, he says, and by the time he takes one out hunting it will have met every type of obstacle and become confident with it already.

More recently, racing has come back into Paul's life through helping a friend, successful builder Luke Comer, who trains a number of mainly flat racehorses, and the venture has got off to a flyer.

Luke bought a colt called Kargali, sold out of John Oxx's yard at the end of the 2009 season at Goffs Sales. By Invincible Spirit, the grey had notched a second and two wins from his three runs as a three-year-old, and the following year, 2009, he was third in the Group 3 Gladness Stakes on the Curragh and won a Listed race in Leopardstown. He suffered from a recurring back problem, and so it was decided to send him to the dispersal sale. Paul recalls that Mick, who mostly rode Kargali for his old boss, said before the sale, 'If you can get him right, he's got a big engine.' Luke Comer paid €52,000 for him, and before spring 2010 was out the horse had already won more than his purchase price, a healthy €60,000. He began by finishing third on the Dundalk all-weather track in February, and then a big weight kept him fairly anchored in the Irish Lincolnshire. In April, he turned out for another crack at the Group 3 Gladness Stakes on the Curragh, with Johnny Murtagh in the saddle. The favourite was John Oxx's Rayeni, who had finished second to Mastercraftsman in the 2009 Irish Guineas, but in the heavy ground that he loves it was 10–1 shot Kargali who romped home to beat the favourite.

Stepping up to the Group 1 Lockinge Stakes at Newbury on much firmer ground in May 2010 proved just too much against the likes of Paco Boy, although he was not disgraced. 'We walked the course beforehand and knew our fate, but the ground was safe, and he came home sound.' Paul added, 'I think there is a Group 1 in him, he's still improving in himself – what's more, he's a colt with a stallion's pedigree. It's great for Luke to get his turn – he's put a lot of money into racing.'

Kargali, who runs in the colours of Mrs Margaret Comer, is not the only highly thought-of Comer horse, and in fact Paul and Luke consider their stable star to be Royal and Regal, for whom at one time they harboured Champion Hurdle hopes. He was also entered in the Irish St Leger but will miss 2010 and is then likely to go back to flat racing. He ran in just one hurdle race, and, while outside eyes were on Royal and Regal, it was the stable's King's Bastion who won.

Paul's enthusiasm remains unabated, and the signs augur

well for the future. And, like the rest of his family, Paul is fiercely proud of his famous brother.

10

Tommy's racing nephews

Michael's son, Chris (b. 1957)

C hris Kinane, known to those close to him as Red from the colour of his hair, had just had a session in the hydro-pool and was lying on his bed exhausted, but he was more than willing to talk. It is five years and a dozen brain operations since the accident. Chris was assistant trainer for Ian Williams and was at a run-of-the-mill Midlands meeting with one runner, carrying out equally run-of-the-mill duties. 'I was in the parade ring in Wolverhampton, and another trainer's horse lashed out and kicked me in the head. I thank my lucky stars that I'm here to talk about it.'

He also thanks his lucky stars for his wife, Tessa, whose life was also turned upside down by the events on that April day in 2005. The couple live in Pulborough, West Sussex, close to where Chris spent his working life – twenty years with Guy

Harwood, and, when Guy switched to the flat, a further five or six years with Josh Gifford at Findon, the stables made famous originally by Ryan Price. Here, on top of the South Downs, riding out in good weather is like being on top of the world, the vast expanse of ancient turf spread out in folds. On a wet and windy or freezing morning it is little short of bleak, but for training a racehorse it ranks among the very best.

As a boy growing up in Hertfordshire, and with his father, Michael, moved on from Chris's mother, his third wife Gill, Chris was only vaguely aware of his family in Ireland. He hunted just once as a child – 'my mother was against it, and you didn't cross her' – yet he knew from an early age that he wanted to be a jockey.

'My brother Alec was born within the sound of Bow Bells and is an artist who is marvellous at carving horses, especially rocking horses. I have some in our garage waiting for our grandchildren.' That was as close as horses came into Chris's family – he also has two half-brothers, Jim and Mick, and two half-sisters, Alice and Jenny – but when his mother Gill married Roddy Ivens, a wealthy importer of tropical fruit, life took a new turn for Chris. 'I sat ten O levels but only got one, and Roddy sent me to boarding school, at Bethany near Goudhurst in Kent. I loved it. There was sport every day, it was an easy regime, and I was caned an awful lot but deserved it.'

In the Easter holidays, Chris visited trainer John Hooton in Sussex and spent the mornings riding out, on the South Downs, across the top of the Long Man of Wilmington (which is carved into the chalk hillside), and in the afternoons he revised for his remaining nine O Levels. He passed them all.

Chris was keen to return in the summer holidays, but John Hooton was shortly to retire, and his advice was to write to an up-and-coming trainer who was 'getting a few winners'. The trainer he suggested was Guy Harwood, a little further along the Sussex coast. Chris wrote, and Guy accepted, but a surprise was in store. 'I am very tall,' says Chris, 'and when I arrived, Guy Harwood strode across the lawn and asked, "Who the hell are you?"' On hearing, Guy said, 'You'll never make a jockey.' It was 1977, and Chris spent the next twenty years there, and from about 700 career rides he rode between eighty and ninety winners.

He also managed to reconnect with his father after a gap of many years. He saw that his uncle, Tommy Kinane, was due to ride Monksfield in the 1976 Triumph Hurdle at the Cheltenham Festival, and Guy Harwood's jockey, Chris Read, was riding at the meeting. Chris Kinane gave Chris Read a letter to give to Tommy, saying he would like to get back in touch with his father. 'Tommy wrote back with Michael's address and said he knew he'd love to hear from me. Then he added, "Welcome to the family." I owe a lot to Tommy.' It resulted in father and son having an emotional reunion at Dublin Airport. 'I knew straight away it was my father. We embraced, and he nearly crushed me! We were both holding back our tears.'

Chris had his first race ride on a horse called Lacrimally in an opportunity hurdle run at Lingfield in March 1977 and finished unplaced. Six months later he rode a horse called Ardent Portion in an opportunity hurdle run at Fontwell in September 1977 and finished a close-up fourth. The Surrey track of Lingfield was also the scene of his first winner Hard Outlook.

It was thanks to Andrew Wates that Chris won for him on Southern Lad. Andrew had bought the horse to hunter-chase but found him too headstrong at home. 'One day Guy asked if I was free on Saturday afternoons and would I like to hunt the horse a few times to get him qualified for hunter chases. The owner rewarded me by promising me a race ride. Southern Lad really got me going. He was a pig of a horse but was very successful.' Subsequently trained by Chris Read, the pair won at Huntingdon on 7 April 1979 in a 2½-mile handicap chase at odds of 20–1.

Better, much better, was to come. Chris's first riding visit to Cheltenham brought a memorable first and last race double in both divisions of a novice hurdle, for owners Sir Ronald Wates on Fredo and for footballer Sir Stanley Matthews on Bravo of Venice, on 24 October 1979.

Chris was still a 7-pound claimer at the time, but more riding successes followed, and he lost his riding claim in 1980. He moved to Josh Gifford for a spell to get a career in race riding, and he was at the Findon stable when the formerly broken-down Aldaniti and jockey Bob Champion, back from the brink of death from cancer, won the fairytale 1981 Grand National.

His best win of all came, memorably, at Cheltenham on New Year's Day 1982 on board Pillager. Usually ridden by stable jockey Richard Rowe, Chris took advantage of his opportunity in the 4-mile chase. He managed to avoid the trouble at the twenty-second fence where two horses fell and brought down a third, leaving him to win unchallenged by thirty lengths.

He returned to Guy Harwood's in 1983 to become assistant trainer with Geoff Lawson and moved on when Guy's daughter Amanda (Perrett) took over. He spent a short spell as racing manager to one of the owners in 1995 and then had six years at Geoff Hubbard's in Suffolk training a string of approximately thirty horses. This was his dream job, and Chris loved every minute of it. When Mr Hubbard died, Chris went to Ian Williams as an assistant trainer up until the fateful day of his accident.

During the period Chris was first at Guy Harwood's, his best mate was going out with a girl called Tessa, but Chris didn't think he treated her very well. He quietly asked Tessa one night if she would go out with him if it was OK with her boyfriend, and she agreed. 'So then I asked my mate if I could ask her out. "No problem," he replied, "She wouldn't go out with you, anyway!" We were engaged for two years, and we've been married for twenty-nine years and never looked back. Tessa was only sixteen years old when we met. I have known her in total for thirty-three years.'

It is ironic that the accident that put Chris in a wheelchair happened not from a fall but when both his feet were on the ground. 'I was building up my riding career, which included crashing falls, and I didn't want to end up in a wheelchair, so I packed up race riding when we had our first daughter.'

Tessa is a great source of strength to him, as are their daughters – Claire (twenty-six) and Michelle (twenty-four) – Tessa's sister Angela and her father Gerry. Angela says, 'Chris is a very lucky man to have Tessa and a strong marriage. There are many frustrations, but there are lots of laughs as well.'

'Red' Chris certainly has that Kinane family trademark: grit.

Dan's sons: Jimmy, Tom and Martin

Jimmy (b. 1950)

Although Jimmy was born when his father Dan was training in Kanturk, County Cork, and was a toddler when he was training for Jack Lombard at Goolds Cross near Cashel, it was at the old rectory, at Mullinahone, that he remembers growing up. He was surrounded by horses, and he was always going to be a jockey. At fifteen years of age he was apprenticed to his father, and on his first ride, on Shuil Osheen, he was beaten a neck.

When Jimmy cantered down to the 1½-mile start at Mallow (now Cork) for about his eighth ride, it was 1966, and he was fifteen years old. The filly, Shuil Osheen's half-sister Shuil Aroon, whipped round, and the young jockey found himself deposited ignominiously on the grass. His uncle Christy, the trainer, cadged a lift in the ambulance in pursuit of the horse. As the remaining runners circled at the start it gave Jimmy, who was hopping around on one leg, time to recover. Christy finally caught up with the filly in the back straight, hurried back to the start and legged Jimmy back into the saddle.

Jimmy weighed only 5 stone 7 pounds and was riding the bottom weight, reduced further by his claim, down to 7 stone. In a fairytale end, Jimmy beat Charlie Weld's runner, ridden by Australian Larry Johnson. A few days later, Jimmy dished up the goods again, without any pre-race mishaps, on Shuil Osheen.

It was a flying start to his career, but Jimmy rode as a professional for only six or seven years, including a six-month spell with Bob Turnell in England. He had about twenty rides for him but homesickness got the better of him, and he returned to Ireland. He rode mostly for his father Dan and uncle Christy but also for Charlie Weld and for some trainers in the north. Jimmy rode seventeen or eighteen winners all told, plus 'an awful lot of slow old yokes'. Jimmy adds, 'As Fred Winter used to say, "If you ride a great race and you're beaten, you're a loser, but it you ride a bad race and win, you're great."'

A mare that Jimmy 'got on great' with was Just Jo. Together they won six races, beginning with a 1-mile-6-furlong maiden flat race in Gowran, beating the hot favourite of Tom Costello's. She also won some hurdles. His last win with her was a novice chase in Limerick in 1972 when she beat the favourite who was trained by Dan.

Although Dan had names such as Flyingbolt pass through his hands, his daughter Eileen's husband's family was responsible for breeding Gold Cup hero Denman, one of the most exciting steeplechasers of recent times and never far from the racing headlines for his successful return to racing from a heart problem and for his amazing ongoing rivalry with his next-door stable companion Kauto Star.

Tom (24 May 1954–January 1984)

Jimmy's brother Tom, the middle of Dan's three sons, was blessed with the Kinane trait of good hands and fine horsemanship. He was also one of the most kind-hearted of men, and, in a life that was cut tragically short at the age of thirty, he was known as a fun character. His cousin Thomas says, 'Tom would do anything for anyone. If someone wanted a tenner off him and he only had a fiver, he would find the extra five somehow.' His uncle Tommy adds, 'He was a class rider, and he was also a champion boxer.' He was on the point of winning an All Ireland championship when he made the youthful mistake of overconfidence and, believing he had it in the bag, was caught off guard, and knocked down. Tom rode for his father Dan and also for Bob Turnell in England. Bob's son, Andy, who was to train Grand National winner Maori Venture in 1987, was first jockey, but Tom had a number of rides and wins. One of his most memorable rides was in the Topham Trophy over the Grand National fences. Riding Eyecatcher for trainer John Bosley, the pair fell at the Canal Turn.

Martin (b. 9 November 1955)

Dan's youngest son Martin has one of those attitudes to life that make him always cheerful company. He rode as a jockey for many trainers, and, one after another, he refers to them as brilliant people. There was only one, who stopped him taking outside rides, that he glosses over, but even then he refers to him as still a friend.

He is also, naturally, full of praise for his cousin Mick. 'He's a fantastic jockey and a credit to his profession. Anyone would like to be as successful, and it's great to see him go out on a high. Sea The Stars was a very, very lucky horse for him.'

Martin grew up in County Tipperary and was not yet fifteen years old when he went to Willie Robinson on the Curragh as an apprentice. Willie is best remembered as the rider of the great Mill House, Arkle's main rival in the 1960s, when he was stable jockey for Fulke Walwyn in Lambourn, Berkshire.

Martin describes Willie Robinson as a 'lovely, lovely' man who treated his apprentices better than most. Typical wages at the time were about £2 or £3, 'but he gave us more'. In addition, Willie's wife, Susan, would meet the lads in Newbridge and buy them suits, jackets – 'anything we wanted'. Their lodgings were better than for lads in many other yards. In other words, 'they treated us like people.'

While Martin was there, the stable produced the 1971 winner of the Irish 2,000 Guineas, Kings Company, owned by Bertram Firestone. Martin also rode his own first winner, a

Above: Brown's Barn in full flight, ridden by Jayo Kinane in the Powers Gold Cup at Fairyhouse.
Below: Aintree Grand National 1988, a perfect shot of Jayo Kinane riding Polly's Pal (number 32) over Becher's Brook; his cousin Martin Kinane was also in the race, riding Brass Change.

Above: The race-riding careers of Tommy and his three eldest sons overlapped: (l-r) Thomas, Tommy, Mick and Jayo.
Below: Mick's first win, aged fifteen, on Muscari, at Leopardstown on 19 March 1975.

Above: 'Going, going – not gone!': Thomas Kinane nearly falling from Segaham Dam in Mallow, but in typical Kinane style he made a fine recovery. The horse was trained by Christy Snr and owned by Dom McParland.

Below: Thomas winning on Smoke Charger, a family favourite, at Thurles. Trained by Tommy, he was ridden by several members of the family and won thirteen races before breaking a leg.

Above: Jayo on Mahler at Ballydoyle, led by his son, Dean, on Song of Hiawatha: 'magic'.
Below: Brendan Kinane on Charante River.

Above and left: Paul showing off hunters for sale.

Top: Mona and Christy Kinane in relaxed mood.

Centre: The Irish Racegoers Club visits Sea The Stars at Gilltown Stud.

Bottom: Christy and Mart Kinane in Cashel, 2010.

Above: Sea The Stars and Mick Kinane winning the Tattersalls Millions Irish Champion Stakes at Leopardstown in 2009; the fifth Group 1 victory in a row for trainer John Oxx.

Left: Mick and Sea The Stars after winning the 2009 2,000 Guineas at Newmarket.

Left: Mick Kinane, no longer in the familiar riding kit, is interviewed by Rishi Persad at the 2010 World Cup meeting in Dubai, four months after his retirement from race-riding.

Below: Tommy with his daughter, Susan, and trainer Jim Bolger enjoying the racing in Dubai.

never-to-be-forgotten experience in a jockey's career. It was at Bellewstown, in north County Meath, a 'holiday' course used then only once a year. It was Martin's eighth ride in a race on a horse called Snowmoss in a 5-furlong event for trainer Danny O'Donnell. Adding to the gloss was that the win was unexpected.

It was while he was an apprentice with Willie Robinson, from 1970 to 1975, that Martin spent three months one winter riding in South Africa, a fantastic experience for the lad. He was out there, in Johannesburg and Durban, with Declan Gillespie, and he placed a good few times in thirty or forty races without winning. 'It was so hot that we would be out on the track at 5 a.m. until 8.30 a.m., and that was the finish of our day's work – we could go swimming, play tennis and at weekends go to a nightclub. In a race, we would canter for a furlong towards the start and then walk, and at the start horses would be given water.'

Martin began to get heavier, and in 1976 he moved to Paddy Sleator's. It was near the end of that respected trainer's career, and jockey Bobby Coonan took over. 'Paddy Sleator was a great man and a good trainer. If a couple of us were sitting down in the yard when he came in he would ask us if we were having a rest. "Yes, boss," we would say. "Oh, you may as well." He knew we had the job done. He also knew when to work his horses and when to leave them alone.'

Martin rode five or six winners there, including a 2-mile flat race in Thurles on King Weasel when Paddy Sleator still held the licence and also the Paddy Power Chase at Fairyhouse on this good horse. Kilbaylet Star was another nice winner for him.

Bobby Coonan, six times Irish National Hunt champion jockey, moved from Grangecon, County Wicklow, to Ballymore Eustace in County Kildare, and Martin rode a few winners for him, but, he says, 'things didn't go Bobby's way. He was a lovely man who seemed to get everything right but didn't get the luck.'

It was time for Martin to move on, and all went swimmingly when he first arrived in England, with John Jenkins in Sussex, as second jockey: he rode five winners in his first twenty-five rides, including three hurdle races on a horse called Easterly Gale, but when John Jenkins moved to Epsom, Martin stayed in Sussex, taking up a post with Lady Herries near the seaside town of Angmering.

During the next five years he rode all her jumpers, and in his career he rode somewhere between 120 and 150 winners. One of the best 'spare' rides came at Wincanton one bank holiday, riding for possibly the greatest National Hunt horseman of all, Fred Winter. His jockey Peter Scudamore had fallen in an earlier race, and Martin picked up his ride in the last on a horse called Baize that gave him a 'fantastic' win, giving him a 100-per-cent strike score for the great man. Martin also rode for, and become lifelong friends with, Peter Jones, who trained at East Kennet, Wiltshire. Not far from him, Martin's brother Tom was riding for Bob Turnell. It was for Peter that Martin rode in the Aintree Grand National and, at the same meeting, won the mares' novice chase final for him on Silent Surrender.

By the early 1990s the outside rides were not so much dry-ing up as were of such poor quality that, in truth, Martin's career was 'gone'. He hung up his saddle but remained in Sussex. He was good friends with Richard Rowe, who packed up race rid-ing the same year and set up training in Storrington, close to his former boss, Josh Gifford, one of the great National Hunt riders, trainers and characters. Martin used to join Richard for lifts to the races, driven by Josh. Sometimes there would be five in the car if jockeys such as Peter Hobbs and Eamon Murphy were also cadg-ing a lift. There was only one thing for certain: the journey would speed by as the young men listened to Josh's stories of derring-do when he was riding and laughed at his reels of jokes. 'He would talk about anything other than the day's riding instructions. He was always fun, and it would take the worry off the day.'

Martin moved with Richard Rowe to be his assistant trainer, and for him the shift was only to 'the other side of the hill' from Lady Herries. Martin worked for five years with Richard Rowe, followed by a brief return to Ireland when his father Dan was ill. Then it was back to West Sussex and to Lady Herries once more as joint head lad for her, along with Dan O'Donovan, sharing the charge of the seventy horses between them. One of their best horses was Celtic Swing, who won the French Derby and was beaten by a head in the 2,000 Guineas in 1995. Another was Taufan's Melody, who won the 1998 Caulfield Cup in Australia. Taufan's Melody was a well-travelled and durable horse who won ten of his forty races. Another star for Lady Herries was Sheriff's Star, who won the

Coronation Stakes of 1989. Lady Herries' sister, Lady Sarah Fitzalan-Howard, had a livery yard in another part of the beautiful grounds of Angmering Park, West Sussex, where Martin also pre-trained a few.

By the turn of the twenty-first century it was time to think about coming back to Ireland permanently – and about getting married. Martin and Theresa tied the knot in the beautiful and imposing Catholic cathedral in Arundel, West Sussex, in 2000. Both Martin's father Dan and his uncle Christy were present.

The couple returned to Ireland in 2001 where Martin completed a RACE (Racing Academy and Centre of Education) training course, became a private trainer in Gort, County Galway, and then bought into South Lodge training establishment in County Tipperary, which had previously seen Phonsie O'Brien and Adrian Maxwell as incumbents. 'I trained a few winners but I didn't have enough good horses to be competitive – there's no chance in Ireland without that. I had one filly that was balloted out nine times. You can't train for the day like that. In the end I just didn't have enough ammunition.'

In some ways, modern-day racing in Ireland has been a victim of its own success, producing too many horses for the amount of races on offer. This leads to huge entries, and if, say, there are 100 entries for a race where the safety limit for the number of runners is twenty, then some eighty horses will be in line for being balloted out.

Martin got out of South Lodge just in time, 'while the Tiger was still running', and 'made a few pounds. It was a fairytale

Kinane: A Remarkable Racing Family

for me and without it I'd be struggling now.' Today, Martin is back in his home county of Tipperary, breaking in yearlings for Michael Woodlock. He enjoys watching Tipperary soccer and hurling and visits Peter Jones, Richard Rowe and Lady Herries each summer – 'I have great memories of England' – and is generally much more relaxed than when he was riding.

To his cousin Thomas he seemed in those days very like Mick: 'quiet, deep and serious, who wouldn't say a lot, but he's come out of himself in the last ten years.' That could have something to do with the fact that, at the age of fifty-four, he now has two young children: six-year-old Colin, who used to love cheering on Mick Kinane when he was riding, and Andrew, born in May 2010.

Jim's son, Tony (b. 1969)

Growing up in Limerick, Tony enjoyed 'messing around' with horses, but although he rode as an amateur for a while it is the breaking and making of young horses that he enjoys most. More of a horseman than a jockey, he went to the UK in 1991, where he worked alongside his cousin Martin for Richard Rowe in Sussex, a county he loved, and for Brian Meehan when he was just starting out in Lambourn.

While in England, Tony had a few rides, and on 19 March 1997, he experienced the thrill of riding into the winner's enclosure. It was not an easy horse, either, for Star Oats was not only a hard puller but was also inclined to make a series of blunders in a race. But on that day at Towcester, when the hunter chase had only four runners, a number that probably helped him, he scored convincingly for trainer Mrs R. M. Lampard and owner Hayden Phillips. It was the second of four rides Tony had on the horse, and he pulled up in the other three after a string of jumping mistakes. In the horse's only other win over fences two years earlier there had been only five runners. His form after that, bar a third next time, consisted entirely of falls, unseats and pulled-ups – and Tony's win.

Today, at the age of forty-one, Tony is part of the team that breaks yearlings for Sheikh Hamdan in Dubai. 'I've been here about seven years. It's nice and relaxed, and I really enjoy the breaking. We have between sixty and 100 each year, and I would break about twenty-five of those.' Tony gets home to Ireland for occasional holidays and family get-togethers, and he recalls the funeral of his father Jim. 'It was more like a party than a funeral, though Billy, my father's twin, was pretty stressed out. Tommy [who is about 5 foot 3 inches] was one of the bearers, but my brothers are 6 feet high and I'm 5 foot 7 inches, and when we came to lower the coffin Tommy nearly fell into the grave with it.'

Of his cousins, Tony says, 'Jayo could have been at the top in jumping, bar that injury, and on the flat Mick was the best I've seen. I don't think there's a breed like him any more – they're not as tough.'

Billy's son, Brendan (b. 6 June 1965)

One glance at Brendan, and you know he's a Kinane: slight in stature, lean, fit – and with that determined Kinane chin. Brendan's life has revolved not only around racing but also around sport in general. He grew up riding ponies on the Curragh where his father Billy worked first for Chally Chute, then Dan Moore and finally Mick O'Toole.

Brendan now lives back within a stone's throw of the original home place in Ballinahinch, in a self-designed dormer house – but he went halfway round the world and back before settling there. Next door is the bungalow that he came to from the Curragh in about 1969 with his parents, Billy and Rose, and sister Anne (now working in Coolmore and married to John Kenrick who used to look after Golden Fleece at Ballydoyle). This is close to where the dynasty began, near the Drehideenglashanatooha Bridge – the longest named bridge in Ireland, Brendan says. Here Brendan, like his cousins, grew up riding ponies, working on local farms, getting up on any horse available even if it meant taking on something deemed 'unrideable', making it and then returning it to its owner as the perfect hunter.

Brendan was also deeply involved in local sport, playing at club level in badminton, soccer, squash, martial arts and, his biggest love of all, running, representing Dundrum AC at lengths up to a marathon. He has also twice cycled the 735 miles around Ireland in aid of the Diabetic Society. 'I'm not going to say horses took a back seat, but they were number two,' Brendan says, 'My interest in horses kindled more in my late teens when I had a few rides.'

Billy was working for Vincent O'Brien at Ballydoyle, and from a young age Brendan was up there whenever he wasn't pursuing one of his other sports. At first, aged about nine, he was only allowed to walk alongside his father on a horse in his summer holidays. The following summer, aged ten, Brendan was allowed to touch the horses, to groom and perform basic tasks, but it was not until he was a young teenager that he was finally allowed to ride any of them. He was about seventeen when his uncle Tommy gave him his first ride in a race, and he finished third in a bumper at Tipperary on Cherryfield, a stalwart member of the stable who was ridden by several Kinanes.

Brendan spent a summer working for Vincent's son David, riding out from 1978, and then worked there full time from 1980 until David quit training. He was part of the team when Assert won both the Irish and French Derbies in 1982. The Epsom Derby was won that year by Golden Fleece, trained by Vincent O'Brien, and Brendan's father, Billy, broke in both horses.

Brendan will never forget the excitement two years later when David's horse Secreto won the 1984 Epsom Derby, beating none other than his father's El Gran Senor, who was favourite. In a thrilling finish, Secreto won by a short head. In spite of this scintillating success, training did not turn out to be David's game, and, in 1988, to the surprise of the racing world, he relinquished his licence and moved into the wine trade. He produced an acclaimed cabernet sauvignon called L'Esprit de Nijinsky from vines planted in 1970, the year of Nijinsky's Classic Triple Crown for his father, Vincent.

Brendan was with him until that time, and then he transferred to Vincent's, where his father Billy still worked, and stayed there for another six or seven years until Vincent's retirement in 1994. It was then a short move to Tommy Stack, who was famous for riding Red Rum to his record-breaking third victory at Aintree and now a very successful trainer. At Tommy Stack's, Brendan rode in a few bumpers, as well as some for his uncle, Tommy Kinane.

But after two years there, along came an opportunity that was to alter his life. 'Some Japanese owners asked if I would go over there for three months to break yearlings for them: I stayed more than twelve years. Japan is an unbelievable country. It's probably the country nearest to being on another planet it is so different. It has held on to old customs and traditions, a bit like Ireland – as islands usually do – and yet Japan's technology is so far advanced that we're unlikely to see it here for another ten years.'

Brendan spent his first two years near Tokyo and then moved to the northernmost island of Hokkaido, which is Japan's main racing base. The spectacular mountainous scenery also draws summer tourists, in spite of the area being on a tectonic plate. 'There were many tremors, and I witnessed a few earthquakes,' Brendan says, 'but the houses were built to withstand them.' He learnt to speak Japanese, something that occasionally comes in useful with Japanese lads at Aidan's now. 'They speak good English, but sometimes if a point needs emphasising I can make it in Japanese.'

For the last seven years of his time in Japan, Brendan was joined by his girlfriend Ruth, who also rode work. Before he went to Japan, she used to ride out for Christy Kinane. One day, Brendan was taking a runner to Dundalk for Vincent. In those days Vincent rested the horses overnight in his stables in the Phoenix Park, and it was when Brendan went out to a shop that he 'spotted the girl from Cashel'.

Towards the end of his stay in Japan, in 2005, Brendan suffered a fall that could have ended his working life. A colt reared over backwards and came down on top of him, shattering his pelvis in three places. Naturally enough, he did not want to worry his mother, Rose, but this involved some subterfuge. He wasn't allowed to use a telephone in the hospital, but she was used to him ringing several times a week. However, he had his mobile phone tucked away. 'I would tell the nurse I needed a bed pan so she would pull the screen around, then I would turn on the tap in the sink, and, while the water was running, I would ring my mother. I told her I'd pulled a muscle in my back.'

In fact, Brendan has yet to sit on a horse again, but he is back to full fitness both for running and work. He reckons the best horses he ever rode work on were College Chapel (Vincent O'Brien's last Royal Ascot winner), the Irish 2,000 Guineas and Breeders' Cup Mile (turf) winner Royal Academy and, in Japan, Tap Dance City, which won the Japan Cup on dirt.

Brendan returned home in 2005 – having built his dormer

house next to his parents' bungalow 'over the Internet' while in Japan. He and Ruth still have many friends in Japan and sometimes return for a holiday. The day Aidan O'Brien's colt George Washington won his first race (22 May 2005 on the Curragh) was the day Brendan landed his job with Aidan. Although George Washington won the first Classic of 2006, the English 2,000 Guineas, luck did not go his way. At the end of the season, after only one more win, he retired to stud, but he was found to be 'firing blanks', and so he was returned to training as a four-year-old, reappearing in June. He placed without winning and, in the autumn, travelled to America for the Breeders' Cup Mile (on dirt). Already out of contention, he broke a leg and had to be put down.

Other than downsides like that, Brendan Kinane clearly loves every minute of working at Ballydoyle, being both dedicated and a workaholic and, as one of the few non-riders, he quickly became involved on the organisational side. After just one and a half years he had become head lad of the Old Main Yard where most of the Classic-bred three-year-olds are stabled.

He is first to arrive at 5.30 each morning, feeding the horses in his yard, making sure that everything is in order, seeing to the bandaging of certain horses' legs, organising the swimming pool, checking the different gallops to be used that day. On 'work' days, he sees to the different jockeys being changed over onto set horses. There are nearly sixty riders, but if anyone is off sick or injured then Brendan will find a replacement. The 'boss' does the 'board', that is, the list of who is going to ride what horse and in which 'lot'. The first 'lot' (string of horses) will pull out of the yard at 8 a.m. or as early as 6 a.m. if the stable has runners abroad that day. Before riding out, the horse's stable will have been mucked out, his hooves picked out and any dust or dirt removed from his coat, mane and tail. Then he is tacked up, and out they go, walking round the quadrangle of the Giant's Causeway yard until the signal to move off is given. Generally there are three lots, taking up the morning, but sometimes a fourth is held in the afternoon.

Most of the lads finish at 5 p.m., and Brendan will be one of the last to leave. 'I love it, and the adrenalin rush. It's like Heathrow Airport without a control tower, organising everything at ground level.'

Once home, it is straight off for a run of anything between 7 and 12 miles, along the lanes and byways where his father hunted a pack of beagles for many years and where all the family grew up. Brendan is often accompanied by fellow runner Michael Ryan, a friend in whom he has the greatest trust. They enjoy diverse conversations while running – on almost any subject other than running or racing. Michael Ryan and Brendan's martial-arts friend John Foley 'acted like brothers to me when my father died'. Billy died in September 2009, and, with his passing, Brendan lost 'not only my father but also my best and closest friend in life.'

Brendan became, and remains, very good friends with Kieren Fallon from the time they worked together in Ballydoyle. He persuaded Kieren to join him up to five nights a

week to play badminton, squash or to go running, to occupy
the talented jockey after he had finished riding work in the
mornings. 'Then at weekends I would book a court for 9 p.m.,
to help keep him on the straight and narrow, to try and keep
him away from drink, drugs, bad company.' Like his father,
Brendan is a Pioneer and has never tried alcohol. 'I've seen the
wrong effects it can have on a person, all the many marriage
break-ups and accidents.'

Of his cousin Mick, Brendan says, 'Everyone said when
he retired it was the end of an era – but there might be another
Kinane champion yet, you never know.'

Sometimes when Ballydoyle has a Group 1 runner abroad
Brendan is called upon to go to the races, but he doesn't always
know in advance. He has got what follows down to a fine art. 'I
can now shave, shower and change into a suit in twelve minutes,' he says, then it is into a top-of-the-range Saab driven by
Aidan, and they are soon in Cork Airport and on their way. It
is a 50-minute flight in a private jet, along with the jockeys, to
the UK, 'one of the perks of the job.' Sometimes on Derby Day
they may accompany John Magnier in his plane. The lads will
have gone with their horses on an earlier flight, Aidan preferring
them to be in their own stables, with the water and food they are
used to, instead of spending the night away, which might also
lead to fretting. In the evening the process is reversed. 'I can be
in the UK at 5.30 p.m. on a Saturday and escorting my mother
to mass in Knockavilla by 7.30 p.m.,' says Brendan.

'It is amazing to have so many good horses but at the same

time they are taken for granted to a certain extent so that we don't let fame interfere with reality.'

Ruth, too, is employed at Ballydoyle, as was her grandfather, Johnny Stapleton, who was head lad to Vincent O'Brien in his earliest 'jumping' days and 'a wonderful handler of young horses'. One of the horses he looked after was Early Mist, winner of the 1953 Aintree Grand National.

One of the first horses Ruth looked after was Dylan Thomas, a colt by Danehill, who won his first two races (of four) as a two-year-old and won the Derby Trial at Leopardstown on his debut as a three-year-old. Although beaten into third in the Epsom Derby (by Sir Percy), hopes were high for Ireland's showpiece, the Irish Derby at the Curragh. It was 2 July 2006, and Ruth wished jockey Kieren Fallon and Dylan Thomas well as she let them off to canter down the course to the 1½-mile start.

She returned to the paddock, where Brendan joined her, and together they watched the race unfold: Dylan Thomas settled into mid-division of the thirteen runners and moved closer as they turned into the straight. Two furlongs out he was third, and then, showing great class over the last furlong, 'her' colt forged clear for an impressive victory. Brendan promptly flung his arms around her – and asked her to marry him. 'Yes!' came the quick reply as she ran off to go and greet 'her' horse and lead him into the special Derby Day winner's enclosure. It was a double celebration for the couple that night, and, just over a year later, in September 2007, they were married in Holy Cross

Abbey, held their reception in Dundrum House Hotel and enjoyed three days in Italy. Later, in the winter 'close' season, they visited Japan and Australia for their honeymoon.

Christy's son, Christy (b. 24 April 1969)

Christy's son, also called Christy, is well remembered as a good amateur and also as something of a practical joker. There is a story that when he was at school, aged about nine, he joined in the fun of swapping sweets – with a difference. He found a quantity of laxative chocolate, probably used by his father to help him waste for low racing weights, and generously doled it out to his friends. They were so busy gorging themselves that they didn't notice he wasn't eating any. The children got a bad dose of the runs, and the parents were up in arms!

Christy grew up at the Green, Cashel, where his father trained, and now, living nearby, he pops in most days to see his mother Mona. From his earliest years he was always around the horses, and before long was riding them. 'I always wanted to race,' he says. He started in pony racing and demonstrated his innate prowess by booting home about 150 winners.

When he left school Christy had a spell in America riding work with Carl Nafzger in Hot Springs, Arkansas, an experience he describes as 'OK, but a bit country and western'. He enjoyed it more when he moved to Keeneland and rode track work there – but one suspects he was longing to be home and applying for his amateur riding licence. He rode his first winner on Isthatafact in an amateur riders' flat race at Naas. The gelding was owned by Peter Gormley, who, as we have seen earlier, pulled off a good win in Limerick Junction on Grand National Day. Unfortunately, the horse suffered from recurring tendon trouble, and eventually Peter Gormley gave him to Christy.

One of the most exciting horses Christy ever rode in work at home was the filly Flower from Heaven, one of Christy Senior's few flat race horses, who won six sprints. 'She was very, very fast. She would jump into a gallop from a standing start, leaving shavings flying in her wake,' Christy remembers. 'She bred a few winners too.'

Christy's first ride in a hurdle race brought a win. It was in Punchestown on a horse called Willyoustop for the late Michael Ahern of Fethard, County Tipperary. His biggest win came in the Galway Blazers Handicap Chase on Arctic Gossip for Matty Cahill of Thurles. It was a race that Christy Senior had also won, and, for Christy Junior, it was a highlight. 'It was a great thrill. Being the Festival there was a big crowd and atmosphere – you don't get that at little meetings.'

Christy rode a good few point-to-point winners and a total of seventeen on the track. Today, he breaks in two-year-olds and rides them in the breeze-up sales for consignor Con Marnane of Bansha, County Tipperary.

Ned's sons: Edmond and Daniel

Edmond (b. 9 October 1966)

Unusual among the Kinane family – Mick excepted – is Ned's son Edmond, whose main love is for flat racing, although, almost inevitably, it was the jumping game and hunting that surrounded him as a child. He spent the first few years of his life in Limerick when Ned was working for (and fishing with) Lord Harrington. Here he learnt to ride at about six years of age on Lady Harrington's 14.2-hand grey pony, Frankie, who had originally started Tommy Carmody and other youngsters off. Out hunting, Lady Harrington would hunt the pony for much of the day and then hand him over to Edmond.

Edmond was nine or ten when he moved with his parents to Crohane, where Ned worked with his brother Tommy. From then, it was a normal part of Edmond's life to ride out on the racehorses and do stable and farm chores along with his cousins, Thomas, Jayo and Paul, each morning before going to school. Mick had already gone to the Curragh, and Daniel, twenty years Edmond's junior, was not yet born.

Edmond was only thirteen when he left school (he was fourteen the coming October) and began full-time work for David O'Brien at the time when stable star Assert (Irish and French Derbies 1982) was one of the world's top racehorses. At sixteen, Edmond had his first race ride when Tommy put him up on Crohane Chieftain. They finished a promising fourth at

Limerick Junction. 'I then had a second on him at Limerick and several more seconds but he was a bit of a boy, codding us. He won a few times when I had left for England!'

Times were tough, and money was bad, though the O'Brien wages were better than most – 'but there were more opportunities in England, and although I'm 5 foot 11½ inches I really wanted to race.'

It was to trainer Pat Mitchell, initially in Polegate, Sussex, that Edmond moved. Pat had many successes with two-year-olds. Edmond had only been there about a year when Pat suffered an accident that confined him to bed for two months. His wife Barbara then had a nasty fall coming out of the trial stalls which saw her laid up for even longer. So it was the staff – head lad Tony and his young crew Meredith, the Mitchells' son Nick and his friend Andy Honeywell (both aged fifteen) and sixteen-year-old Edmond who not only kept the show on the road but also produced a good number of winners as well. 'We were basically a bunch of kids who kept it going, and, actually, it was about Pat's best season,' Edmond remembers. 'There was one particularly good horse called Irish Sailor who sluiced in at Newmarket in a big handicap and then did it again a week later.'

Pat sold up in Sussex and moved to Hamilton Road in Newmarket when Edmond was twenty-two. A number of owners asked Edmond if he would train for them, and to this day he regrets turning them down. Instead, he worked for a year for Alex Stewart in Newmarket where Mtoto was the stable star. He won the Eclipse and the King George and was second in the Arc.

'I love the flat, and I love flat horses – they're amazing creatures. I get more of a buzz and love their characters. They're temperamental yet easier to manage than jumpers because they're so young, and they learn quickly. Jumpers need time and often get leg problems.'

Edmond himself had between forty and fifty rides, mostly on the flat and a few over hurdles. His first ride in England was in Ascot, no less. 'The number-board people didn't have my name, and, as I rode out I glanced up and saw what they had put instead: M. J. Kinane! It was a brilliant day, and a lovely track. On another occasion I also had a ride in a 1½-mile amateur flat race at Goodwood, equally lovely.'

But that special moment of riding into the winner's enclosure for the first time eluded him, though in July 1988, when he was back in Ireland, he was particularly unlucky. 'I had several rides booked for the Galway Festival, and I was really hopeful.'

The Sunday before, Edmond was messing around with his cousins as usual, playing a game of five-aside football, when he turned his ankle over. He was on crutches for some weeks and watched in disbelief as the first of his intended mounts, Try a Brandy, scooted home on day one and promptly turned out again three days later to win the prestigious Galway Hurdle no less. Another intended mount on the first day, Pandora's Magic, finished third in the bumper.

Of the family five-aside, Edmond says, 'Whether it's football or hurling we kill each other. Such is life.'

Edmond went off to the valleys of South Wales and trained point-to-pointers for a year and then, perhaps even more surprisingly, took a spell out of racing altogether and worked as a security guard in Kensington Mews, London. On only his second night on duty he spotted a sporty silver Ford driving fast towards the barrier. No way was he going to let that through without checking, so he flagged it down and walked over. The driver wound down the window and spoke to him. It was Princess Diana! 'She asked me my name and spoke for four or five minutes with me.'

Today, back in Ireland, and after a ten-year spell working at Coolmore Stud, Edmond has teamed up with his cousin Paul in helping Luke Comer with his horses. They also have a nice three-year-old colt that they bought for Tottenham Hotspur footballer David Bentley. By Spartacus, the colt's dam is Unaria, who has bred two listed race-winning fillies already, Edmond says. 'She has bred nine winners from eleven runners. Richard Hannon has a half-brother who has won sixteen races, and this colt is the best bred of the lot.' He also has a well-related filly whose family he has known for many years. 'We didn't run her but named her Dancing with Stars, before Sea The Stars had come on the scene. She's in foal to Excellent Art, and I hope she's going to be lucky. You have to be an optimist,' he says.

Daniel (b. 1986)

Edmond had already moved to England when Daniel was born,

Kinane: A Remarkable Racing Family

twenty years his junior. Daniel never raced, but he inherited another Kinane skill: dancing. He was one of the most talented ballroom dancers in Ireland and swept all before him. He won the junior and youth Irish championships with a schoolfriend, Lisa Cochrane, and, as an adult, he partnered a Russian dancer, Olga Kozlov, to win the All Ireland Open Ballroom Dancing Championship. The pair also danced for Ireland all over Europe. Yet racing is also in his blood, and, although not a rider, twenty-three-year-old Daniel has become yet another Kinane to work in Ballydoyle – he works as a lad for Aidan O'Brien in the two-year-olds' yard.

11

'As rare as hens' teeth'

The Kinanes at Ballydoyle

Driving through the smart entrance to Ballydoyle, just outside the village of Rosegreen, County Tipperary, one is greeted first by the security guard and then by the bronze statue of Nijinsky, the horse who, perhaps more than any other, put Ballydoyle on the map. Continuing up the tree-lined tarmac road, with white rails and all-weather work areas on one side and stud-railed fields and more roads on the other, it is hard to imagine when this was just like any other piece of Tipperary farmland, criss-crossed by hedges, dotted with dairy cows and with people going about their farming business, hunting and breeding a point-to-pointer or two.

That's how it was when the young Vincent O'Brien bought it in 1950. Before that, Vincent had had the use of his half-brother Donal's stables and gallops in Churchtown, County Cork.

O'Brien bought the original 285 acres of Ballydoyle for £17,000, and he, more than any other Irishman, had the vision to see how it – and racing in Ireland – could be. He knocked holes in hedges, wide enough for horses to gallop upsides two or three abreast, and, after the Cheltenham meeting of March 1951, where he trained Hatton's Grace to win his third consecutive Champion Hurdle, Vincent and his horses moved in. He ploughed his winnings back into his dream, and eventually he brought in partners who were to transform Ballydoyle and Irish racing itself, putting both at the peak of the global racing map.

From 1969, Dennis Hickey acted as secretary and right-hand man, greeting visitors – just as he does today. Over the years, a number of assistant trainers at Ballydoyle have gone on to make successful careers for themselves, but there is one family name that is as a rock in Ballydoyle: Kinane. From the earliest days, Vincent would have a Kinane working for him, beginning with Dan, who worked for him in Churchtown, County Cork.

Billy Kinane arrived at about the same time as Dennis Hickey, and one of his first jobs was breaking and backing the yearlings. Before long, Vincent would have only Billy, and no one else, be the first on a valuable youngster's back, down at the Lyonstown yard (about a mile from Ballydoyle).

Billy rode work on many of the world's most famous

racehorses, as we have seen, and of them all Roberto was his favourite. As a yearling, Roberto had to have a number of warts removed from his body. They did not affect his ability (although his trainer considered his 'flat' knees might), and until his dying day Billy maintained he was the best horse he ever rode.

There was a day when he was to ride work on him at Limerick Junction, and Vincent had sent three or four sprinters along to lead him. They started five lengths ahead of Roberto over what was only a sprint distance of 4½ or 5 furlongs – but Roberto finished five lengths in front of them. Roberto won three races in Ireland as a two-year-old in 1971 and went on to win the Epsom Derby by the narrowest of margins the following year in the hands of Lester Piggott.

Brendan says, 'My father always said he was the fastest of all the good horses, and the best, something he repeated on his deathbed. Vincent used to say my father was the best man he ever saw to ride a two-year-old. It was a massive compliment to someone who worked there for quarter of a century.'

Vincent's successor, Aidan O'Brien, has unsurprisingly continued the Kinane trend. Would-be lads can be queuing tens deep, but if there is a Kinane available it is short odds he will be selected. 'They are unbelievable workers, they are all horsemen and have the greatest integrity,' Aidan says.

If Vincent O'Brien was known for being meticulous down to the last minor detail, then Aidan has managed to put a whole new meaning on the word. Yet his demeanour, while serious, can break into a smile when he relaxes. His staff respects him, and he respects them, especially the Kinanes. Of Jayo, he says, 'He's a superstar, with great experience, and he's a great rider and horseman.' Brendan is 'unbelievable, meticulous and dedicated. Being able to work with people like them is a privilege. We're lucky enough that we can afford that quality of genuine person. They're like hens teeth – special people, and a fine example of the way they were brought up.'

Aidan has known Tommy Kinane since he was a young amateur and rode in bumpers for him when he was training in Crohane. He would spend time there with Tommy and his wife Frances, of whom he became very fond. 'In later years, Mr Kinane used to come here with Mick,' Aidan says, 'and when my children, Joseph, Sarah, Anna and Donnacha, were little he used to play with them on the floor, bucking them off his back, teaching them how to sit a difficult horse.'

Aidan considers Mick Kinane's time at Ballydoyle a dream period. 'It was an absolute high-spot time for me. Week after week there was big race after big race – I think we had something like twenty-three Group 1 winners one year – but Mick was never stressed. If he was worried, I wouldn't know. He was a thorough gentleman, always very quiet – and very wise. He was very strong mentally, a deep thinker – and a thorough professional. He was always a pleasure to deal with – and I don't think I ever saw him have a fall here!'

Aidan tells a story that probably sums up Mick's professional attitude as well as any. It was just before the Irish Derby of 2000, and Mick was due to ride Ciro. The American-bred colt was out of a Nijinsky mare and had won three races, but he finished only sixth in the French Derby and was not expected to win the Irish Derby, as reflected in his 20–1 starting price. Mick had hurt his back but hoped to be back for the Curragh's big day, but the injury did not improve as hoped, and he ran out of time. On the morning of the Irish Derby he rang Aidan: 'Mick literally couldn't get the words out. He was on the phone but nothing was coming out, he was so gutted at letting us down. The horse only had half a chance, but that's how committed he was.' In the event, George Duffield deputised, to finish third behind Sinndar – and in his run after that, Mick won the Secretariat Stakes at Arlington on him.

Of the other Kinanes currently working at Ballydoyle – Ned's son Daniel and Jayo's son Dean – Aidan is equally full of praise. 'Good people are easily managed, and everyone respects each other.' Four men, from a staff of approximately 140, ride out only: Jayo, Sam Curling and joint second jockeys Colm O'Donoghue and Seamus Heffernan. 'Otherwise, everybody does everything.' Part of the ethos at Aidan's is that boxes are sumptuously filled with straw, and there are no horse-walkers (those mechanical 'exercisers' that dispense with staff time): 'They're enough to turn any horse into a zombie,' Aidan says. Instead, the lads take out each horse individually for a pick of grass every afternoon.

Jayo Kinane also has views on equine swimming: 'Developing the swimming muscle too much makes for a short stride and makes a horse get too stocky in the chest muscle, but it's fine combined with terrestrial work and good for conditioning.'

Aidan himself rides out at lunchtime for his eldest son, Joseph, who has a small yard of his own. At the age of sixteen, Joseph is not only carving out a race-riding career for himself but has also been a successful event rider. In May 2010 he was awarded the Irish Field Junior Event Rider of the Year. So, finally, would Aidan consider people like the Kinanes to be the backbone of racing?

'They are much more than that,' is Aidan's immediate response.

12

Mick seeing stars

After the fifteen years at Dermot Weld's, where Mick had grown from boy to man and from domestic champion to world recognition, his move to Ballydoyle proved the start to an eventful four years. They included some of the greatest winners – even by Ballydoyle standards, among them one of the best in Galileo who won the 2001 Epsom Derby, Irish Derby and King George at Ascot and who lost his unbeaten record by only a head against Fantastic Light in a truly memorable Champion Stakes at Leopardstown. (He was then well beaten in America.) By Sadler's Wells out of Urban Sea, it was breeding that was to come significantly into Mick's life again . . .

With Ciro, Mick took the 2000 Secretariat Stakes at Arlington (the horse he had been unable to ride in the Irish Derby because of injury). He also won at the Breeders' Cup three times on High Chaparral (2002 and 2003 Turf) and Johannesburg (2001 Juvenile). Hawk Wing, Giant's Causeway and Rock of Gibraltar were other stars that featured high up on Mick's CV during his time at Ballydoyle. In 2001 alone he rode some seventeen Group or Grade 1 winners.

In the swings and roundabouts of stable jockeys Mick left Ballydoyle just as Johnny Murtagh, following injury, felt unable to commit to John Oxx for the new season. So, in 2004, Mick found himself heading for the comparatively quieter waters of Curraghbeg. John Oxx trains 100 horses from there, yet somehow it is a more 'homely' set-up, and certainly the two men suited each other. For Mick, it was not only close to the lovely home he had built on 80 acres outside Naas – Eadling House (named after his daughters Sinead and Aisling) – but it also gave him the personal involvement that he relished: to be 'making' young horses, sorting through the two-year-olds, picking out the likely future winners – and, in one case, the special one.

Fairytales get written and are generally dismissed as just that, but for Mick Kinane the fairytale of bowing out on the horse of the decade, of the century – possibly *ever* – was to come true.

John Oxx was no stranger to the world's top thoroughbreds, from the great mare Ridgewood Pearl through many others to Epsom and Irish Derby winners Sinndar (2000) and Alamshar (2003). One of the aspects of riding for John Oxx that Mick Kinane enjoyed most was assessing the newly broken two-year-olds. As both men are quiet by nature, neither is given to outbursts of excitement at any particular prospect.

One morning in April 2008, John pointed to a big bright bay two-year-old and asked Mick to ride him. Curious, Mick asked who it was. A half-brother to Galileo, came the reply. Mick was intrigued. He returned from the canter impressed. From that day on, when it came to 'fast work', Mick was on the youngster called Sea The Stars.

Mick found Sea The Stars an easier ride than Galileo. It soon became apparent that the colt had a high cruising speed, smooth change of gear and excellent acceleration. A Ferrari among the Fords, but his temperament was sheer Rolls-Royce – and that was what set him apart. He might have had equals, but no one could have ridden Sea The Stars better than Mick Kinane, in all nine of his races. The 2008 season, when Sea The Stars was introduced to racing as a two-year-old, had been the first time since the mid-1980s that Mick had failed to ride a Group 1 winner. To an outsider, it might have appeared time to quit, to call an honourable retirement. But Mick Kinane had an inkling of something truly special up his sleeve. He went off to Dubai with a spring in his step, belying the fact that he was in his fiftieth year, and he spent the winter months pounding the sunlit streets there, 5 miles at a stretch, ensuring he would be as fit or fitter than jockeys half his age for the summer ahead. Retirement was definitely put on hold for a year.

Mick was to say later that although he had ridden some very good horses, Sea The Stars was the only one he believed capable of winning both a 2,000 Guineas and a Derby. It is surprising to the layman, perhaps, just how much difference half a mile can make in a racehorse: the Guineas, over 1 mile, is for the speedsters – almost sprinters – who are unlikely to have the stamina for the 1½-mile Derby, while the Derby prospects, bred to stay, are unlikely to have the fleetness of foot for the Guineas.

In the preceding four decades before 2009, only two horses had proved capable of the double: Nijinsky and Nashwan. A good many others tried and failed. In May 2009, pundits saw the 2,000 Guineas as a clash between Brian Meehan's Delegator, who was the favourite, ahead of Aidan O'Brien's Rip Van Winkle, Sir Michael Stoute's Evasive and Jim Bolger's Gan Amhras. Sea The Stars, without a previous run that season, was not even a certain starter, because of ground concerns, setting a pattern for much of that incredible summer. Nevertheless, he made the line-up and started at 8–1 with five of the fifteen runners at shorter prices. In the race, at the moment that mattered, Sea The Stars accelerated fast out of the pack in a style that he was to make his own.

The 2,000 Guineas was a stepping stone to the Derby, but Sea The Stars' pedigree did not guarantee him getting the 1½-mile trip. The weather in June 2009 was not going to be hot and sunny: rain was forecast, and John Oxx was not sure if he should let his star run. He was convinced his colt did not want soft ground, which would also put a premium on stamina, but once he had ascertained that the ground was good, he declared him to run.

O'Brien's Fame and Glory was the favourite. About the

only certainty was that the finish would involve Irish horses, for seven of the twelve runners were from Ireland, and five of them headed the bookmakers' list – but not Sea The Stars. Not yet for him superstar status.

There was not long to wait.

Sea The Stars began by pulling wildly, throwing his head up in the air, trying to evade Mick Kinane's efforts to restrain him. Being the horseman he is, Mick soon had him relaxed and running well within himself, but the fear had to be that, given the doubts over his stamina, he would have used up too much energy in fighting early on.

A big horse can find it harder to cope with Epsom's gradients and, in particular, the infamous bend called Tattenham Corner, around which many an immature three-year-old's hopes of immortality have been dashed. Sea The Stars had no such problems for he was perfectly balanced as he galloped round the corner and headed down the hill. From there on, on the heels of the leaders, he never looked in danger and took the lead a full furlong out, looking strong at the finish. All doubts about stamina vanished.

For the man on board the outcome was a foregone conclusion. Mick told the waiting press, 'Every step of the way I was winning today . . . It was never in any doubt. I didn't think anything was going to beat me coming from behind. This horse has given me a new lease of life . . . He was just coasting, he has so much class.'

Behind him, four of Aidan's six runners took second, third,

fourth and fifth places: Fame and Glory, Masterofthehorse, Rip Van Winkle and Golden Sword. In June 2010, Fame and Glory won the Coronation Stakes over the same course and distance.

Sea The Stars was now on his way to winning all six of the races he contested that unforgettable summer of 2009 – every one of them a Group 1. Never again did he run at odds against: he now had superstar status, and, try as they might, other stables simply couldn't throw up a rival to match him. Notable among these was Ballydoyle. There was one occasion when all three of Sea the Star's opponents came from that yard, and, on another, no fewer than five Ballydoyle horses lined up using all the tactics they could to dethrone him. But in Sea The Stars, John Oxx, owner Christopher Tsui, Mick Kinane and the world of racing truly had a great horse in their midst.

In his next race after the Derby, the Coral Eclipse at Sandown over the shorter distance of 1¼ miles, it looked briefly as if challenger Rip Van Winkle might pass Sea The Stars, but moments later the Star franked his class again, overtaking him with ease to score convincingly.

At York, for the Juddmonte International, only three rivals took him on, all from Ballydoyle, and two of those were pacemakers. In this, Mastercraftsman also looked, for a matter of moments, as if he might not be passed, but Mick Kinane knew exactly what he was doing. Able as ever to adapt to circumstances, Mick rode him beautifully to another victory.

Having bypassed the Irish Derby (for weather and ground doubts), won in his absence by Fame and Glory, Sea the Star's adoring Irish racing public at last had a chance to see him in the flesh that summer. This was for the Irish Champion Stakes at Leopardstown and was the occasion on which no fewer than five Ballydoyle horses were lined up against him. Of the nine runners, five of them were priced at 100–1 or 150–1, and only Fame and Glory and Mastercraftsman were featured in the market, with Dermot Weld's Casual Conquest sneaking a look in at 16–1.

It was a marvellous race to watch. Set Sail duly lived up to his name by taking the lead, and by the time the business end of the race was reached, Mastercraftsman assumed the lead, if briefly, before Fame and Glory took over. Might the Irish Derby winner cause an upset? Then along came the champion, racing smoothly past his rivals and taking the lead fully a furlong out. Sea The Stars galloped to a victory that he made look easy. Yet again, Mick had ridden flawlessly.

After the race, an unusually bullish John Oxx called his horse the best by far, adding, 'He'll win the Arc.' And so the scene was set. The Prix de l'Arc de Triomphe at Longchamp was to be Sea The Stars' biggest challenge. The 'Arc', as it is affectionately known, is Europe's richest horse race and is seen as the end-of-season test in which the best from many countries take each other on. No horse had ever won the 2,000 Guineas, the Derby and the Arc (which is open to all ages) in one season.

Now, eighteen opponents lined up against Sea The Stars, Europe's elite along with the usual number of pacemakers. It is a sign of the esteem in which Sea The Stars was now held that after his odds of 4–6 the next nearest was his old rival Fame and Glory on 6–1. Sea The Stars was notably more keyed up than usual, and, when at last they were under way, he could be seen desperately fighting Mick Kinane for his head. It was like the Derby again but worse. Eventually Mick got him settled, but in doing so he was now way back in ninth place against the rail with a host of horses ahead and to the side of him. With a mass of horses surrounding him, could he, when the moment came, not only extricate himself but also have enough speed and stamina to go on and win a race as prestigious as the Arc, or would the other jockeys close him in? Thousands of spectators and worldwide television viewers held their collective hearts in their mouths.

The pacemakers had gone so far clear that in truth the real race was being led by Stacelita, ridden by Christophe Soumillon, and Dar Re Mi with Jimmy Fortune. Sea The Stars was on the inside and looked completely boxed in. But slowly, inexorably, he pulled through the throng to join the leaders. Although it still looked an impossible task, he changed gear again to swoop imperiously past the front runners, leaving them toiling in his wake as he galloped clear to win by two lengths. It was a performance that truly set him apart, one of the greatest moments in horse-racing history. Soon superlatives outdoing superlatives rolled off tongues and pens alike.

For Mick Kinane, used to riding top-flight horses all over the world, Sea The Stars was 'simply the best. An extraordinary talent who [was] a pleasure to ride. A horse that comes along only once in a lifetime.'

There were rumblings and debates about whether Sea The Stars would run in the Breeders' Cup in America, and although Mick stayed true to his commitment to ride abroad, retirement for both of them was inevitable. Nine days after the Arc, on 13 October 2009, it was announced that the world's greatest racehorse would retire to stand at the Aga Khan's Gilltown Stud in County Kildare.

At the Irish National Stud, where Sea The Stars was born, groups of tourists – Japanese, American, Australian, English, Irish – walk round on a blustery autumn day and are informed and entertained by tour leader Tony, who clearly loves his job, his words coming out freshly with no hint that they are repeated three times a day. He proudly talks about the famous horse and how they knew 'from day one' at the stud that Sea The Stars, a colt with a lovely nature, was going to be a star. He had an action, he said, that set him apart so distinctly that when John Oxx came to see him as a yearling his advice to the owners was 'don't sell that one'. Mick Kinane also postponed his retirement for a year in order to ride him, Tony tells the group, as they walk down the avenue between the stallion paddocks.

Later, on the phone, Mick tells me, 'He shouldn't have said that!' and then adds, with masterly understatement, 'It was a great season.'

Nine months after those gruelling 5-mile runs in the heat of Dubai, amid the hectic scenes surrounding the announcement of Sea The Stars' retirement, Mick and his wife Catherine took themselves off for a couple of days to the tranquillity of the river Shannon.

The announcement of his own retirement was almost inevitable and widely anticipated (it eventually came on 8 December 2009), but first, in true Kinane fashion, he honoured his promise to ride in South Africa and Japan.

It was highly appropriate that Mick's last winner was on Nebula Storm, carrying the yellow colours with purple cap and yellow star made so famous by Sea The Stars, in a two-year-old maiden race at Leopardstown on 5 November 2009.

Mick retired, having won ten English classics: the Epsom Derby with Commander in Chief (1993), Galileo (2001) and Sea The Stars (2009); the Epsom Oaks with Shahtoush (1998) and Imagine (2001); the 2,000 Guineas with Tirol (1990), Entrepreneur (1997), King of Kings (1998) and Sea The Stars (2009); and the St Leger with Milan (2001). In Ireland he won fourteen Irish classics as well as a record seven Irish Champion Stakes.

The rewards and accolades for his stupendous season and outstanding career came in thick and fast. Fellow jockeys, trainers, owners and the racing public at large heaped lavish praise on Mick Kinane. 'Michael is without doubt the best jockey that this country has produced,' Brian Kavanagh, CEO of Horse Racing Ireland told the *Racing Post*. 'His record of big race wins speaks for itself as does his loyalty and long service to his employers during his career. Michael changed the way in which Irish riders, and indeed Irish racing, were perceived worldwide and showed that Irish riders can more than hold their own internationally. He paved the way for a generation of Irish jockeys and acts as a wonderful role model for any young apprentice starting out. Professionalism and dedication, allied to a natural modesty, were his trademarks, and throughout his career he was the man with the nerve and talent for the biggest occasion.'

Fellow jockey Pat Smullen, who took over from Mick at Dermot Weld's, said, 'He was the greatest of them all and always my role model, and it was a pleasure to ride against him for the past fifteen years or so.'

Dermot Weld himself described Mick as 'the complete professional. He was world class, and we had many happy and successful years together. He was a great stable jockey, and his all-round talent as a jockey was exceptional. His ability as a brilliant reader of a race was a huge part of his success. He is a very intelligent individual who would have been a success at any role he chose in life.'

For many, including his own family, Mick's retirement spelled the end of an era. He was the complete jockey, and for anyone to emulate him will be difficult in the extreme. He was the last of a long line of Kinane jockeys, and of the next generation very few ride let alone race. Even so, there might be one waiting in the wings.

Mick's family remember him as a light-hearted lad, up for a laugh, but much of the sense of fun was knocked out of him, in public at least, as an apprentice and later with the weight of responsibility on his shoulders. 'He's always been serious,' says Tommy, 'but he will lighten up. It will take time because when you've been at the top of your game for so long you give it your all, and it takes time to wind down again.'

Throughout Mick's career he was a superb ambassador for the sport of racing worldwide and for the thoroughbred industry in Ireland in particular. Just about every jockey award going went his way, including the prestigious Cartier Award in London and many press awards. By the time March 2010 came around, it seemed there was just one more to come – but a surprise was in store.

Monday, 22 March 2010. It is the Keadeen Hotel, Newbridge, a stone's throw from the Curragh, and Mick Kinane is receiving yet another award for his all-conquering 2009 exploits. It is one of the last for Mick as he is presented with the Contribution to the Industry Award by his peers in the training and riding ranks of the Irish Racehorse Trainers Association. Then, unexpectedly, there is another – maybe the most coveted of all. Just when it looks as if formal proceedings are at an end and trophy recipients are lining up for photographers, a delegation of senior jockeys suddenly appears on the stage. Calling on Mick Kinane one more time, Andrew Coonan, Secretary of the Irish Jockeys Association, presents him with a bronze horse and thanks him for 'effectively policing the jockeys' room for thirty years'. Mick is then enrolled as the Association's first Honorary Member.

In May 2010, it was announced by Horse Racing Ireland that Mick Kinane had been appointed to promote Irish flat racing. He is particularly keen to do his bit at increasing attendance figures at race meetings, and this had begun a few days earlier when the Curragh's bank-holiday crowd was double that of the year before – a feat Mick put down to Horse Racing Ireland's hard work. He said, 'We're in challenging times at the minute, and Horse Racing Ireland are working hard to get the word out that we have a great product to sell, a great day's entertainment and social scene. We probably took crowds for granted. People maybe see the flat as a bit elitist, but it's far from it – if you were to see the first three home in the 1,000 Guineas [Newmarket 2010], they were all bargain-basement purchases.'

The role will suit Mick and will tie in nicely with his home life. Eadling House and its acres have matured and are well tended, not least by Tommy, who will often be seen out on a tractor. Situated at Craddockstown, between Naas and Punchestown, it has become a model stud farm. There, the progeny of some of the Group 1 winners that Mick rode graze by day and come in for a good feed at night, guarded by a large brown Alsatian and a smaller cream-coloured one. It was here that Mick bred Authorised, winner of the 2007 Derby, a son of Montjeu on whom Mick won the King George in 1999 and the Arc a year later.

A visitor to the yard is likely to be attended to by one of Mick's family while he is inclined to remain quietly in the background. Mick is unlikely to let himself get unfit, and one of the ways he keeps his hand in is by continuing to ride out for John Oxx a couple of times a week. No doubt these two wise men will mull over the horses' prospects for years to come.

Epilogue

Tommy travels the world

In 1999, Frances and Mick contrived between them to persuade Tommy to retire from both training and riding out, although, he adds proudly, he did win a charity race at Lucky Leopardstown that year, at the age of sixty-six. At about this time, Mick told his parents that there was something he would like to show them. Intrigued, they went with him after racing, and he showed them 80 acres of bare, but obviously good, land at Craddockstown, between Naas and Punchestown. The seeds were sown.

Mick built the lovely Eadling House and, in time, put up the barn-style stables, sand arena, many furlongs of stud railings and dug what was, with maturity, to become a lovely pond. He had a fine house for himself and family, the lodge bungalow at the head of the front drive for his esteemed parents and another one at the back for his older brother, Thomas. And he persuaded his father, finally, to retire.

Tommy was sixty-six years old and confesses, 'I was a bit mad about it at first.' But although he retired from training nothing could or would see him retire completely, and he plays an active role both on Mick's farm and in the stables as well as dancing up to three times a week. 'I feel I belong here in County Kildare now,' he says.

When I first visited Mick's magnificent stables, to view a potential hunter for sale belonging to his youngest brother Paul, there was a 'lad' sweeping the nearly spotless stable yard in the background. We repaired into the tack room for a coffee but no sooner had Tommy downed his than he was back out with the broom. Already a septuagenarian, his work ethos was as undimmed as ever; that, and being a stickler for tidiness, the truth and punctuality are inerasable parts of his make-up. He is not afraid to stand up for his principles, and neither is he one to suffer fools gladly. Now approaching seventy-seven years of age, Tommy is 'fitter than any of us,' his eldest son Thomas remarks, before adding, 'except perhaps Mick.'

In 2000, Tommy and Frances were enjoying a day out in Leopardstown, a 'busman's holiday' for Tommy and scene of so many family successes. Frances filled in the competition inside their race cards, dropped them into the collection box and thought no more about it. That evening there was a phone call from the Emirates. The couple had won an all-expenses-paid holiday to Dubai for the World Cup.

One morning at breakfast in Dubai, as they perused the big race runners, they were approached by a dapper, bearded gentleman. 'Excuse me, Tommy, you don't know me, but . . . ' (the familiar introduction of members of the public to a celebrity). It was Tony Reilly, Secretary of the Irish Racegoers Club. 'Would you do us the honour of joining us today?'

It was the beginning of a long and fruitful relationship, one that has taken Tommy to far-flung places that he might well otherwise never have visited, such as South Africa, Australia, the USA, South America, many European countries and, of course, Dubai. It was while he was on one of these trips that Frances became ill in 2005. A few short weeks later she died of acute leukaemia. It was in June, just before the Irish Derby, and Mick, understandably, did not ride in it.

Tommy goes on many of the Irish Racegoers Club trips, and ten years later, is the Club Chairman. Whenever there was a meeting at which Mick was riding, such as Cologne, for instance, or Longchamp, Mick was sure to pop into the pre-race lunch and offer a few tips to the club members in his quiet, mild manner.

Life will never be the same for Tommy without Frances, but he gives it his best shot, remaining both active and fit, and with a wide circle of friends. At the age of seventy-seven (in October 2010) Tommy still goes dancing a few times a week and receives many propositions from younger women – but it is to his home alone, surrounded by pictures of Frances and the family, that he chooses to go.

Early in 2010 Tommy mentioned to Mick that he would like to ride out. 'Mick just looked at me,' he said, and that was the end of that. 'But I did ride an ostrich when I was on safari in Africa in 2008 – not to mention a camel in Dubai!'

In Dubai in 2010, it was the newly retired Mick who was on holiday, with his wife Catherine, two daughters, Sinead and Aisling, and, of course, Tommy. As they flew in they could see the various man-made islands representing different countries of the world, looking remarkably recognisable in the sea around the city. These were the brainchild of Sheikh Mohammed and were built from sand, covering an area of 6 by 9 kilometres. In the distance they could see the latest 'world's tallest building': the 2,717-foot-high Burj Khalifa, part of the 'skyscraper city'.

The first thing Tommy found at the Old Metropolitan, Dubai's very first hotel, was a badge for the meeting and party invitations from Sheikh Mohammed. It was the first year at the sumptuous, luxurious, no-holds-barred Meydan Racecourse. 'It has changed in a big way,' says Tommy, 'The huge new hotel and grandstand are awesome, brilliant – but I miss the old "party in the desert". It was three times more exciting and homely than the new one because we were closer together then, but otherwise the new one is a great place.'

On the morning of World Cup night 2010, the sun was blazing down outside, but inside the cowboy-themed Rattle Snake Club the air-conditioning kept the members of the Irish Racegoers Club cool. It was their tenth annual visit to the Dubai World Cup. The club ladies were resplendent as ever in their hats and summer dresses. The banter began: 'And next into the paddock is a fine-looking filly, a bit leggy and beautifully turned out, she should cut a dash . . . Now this one is a flaming chestnut, she looks to have the better of the groom leading her round, she might be a sprinter . . . Ah, here's one that might stay the distance, pretty hat on her head and a good behind, too.' There was a titter of laughter. The irrepressible Tommy Kinane – who else?! – was compèring the annual hat competition among the ladies. The winner was Kathleen Keating, of County Meath.

Then it was off to enjoy the Breakfast with the Stars. Beautifully laid tables stretched for half a mile on the lawns each side of the winning post, ten people to a table. It is a tradition that has quickly become a part of the meeting and adds to the atmosphere. Here Tommy and people like him greeted old friends from all over the world. It was like an Old Boys' reunion, meeting up again with trainers, owners, jockeys, press and racing dignitaries.

The sweltering heat had cooled a little as dusk fell, and the first race of the eight-race card, worth a staggering US$26.25 million, took place as the floodlights shone down onto the acclaimed Tapeta surface, designed by Michael Dickinson. Based in America but forever remembered for training the first five home in the 1983 Gold Cup, headed by Bregawn, a foray into training for the flat did not prove a success, but Dickinson's move to Maryland did, and there he became the respected and successful trainer he deserved to be. Gradually he built up a reputation not only for training but also as a businessman, and

Kinane: A Remarkable Racing Family

the success of his Tapeta surface, after painstaking trial and error, sees him travelling worldwide and enjoying the recognition he has earned.

Dickinson was there, along with the great and the good of the mostly flat-racing world. A crowd of some 50,000 enjoyed the early races and the build-up to the US$10-million World Cup, but first there was to be a monumental firework display. In order not to frighten the fourteen contenders, already on their toes and tuned to the minute, the horses remained in the dark, cool tunnel until the display was over. Only then, as they entered the paddock, did they feel the heat for the first time – for even their stables were air-conditioned.

The fifteenth running of the Dubai World Cup over 1 mile 2 furlongs produced a finish as exciting as any horse race can be, so tight that no one was sure of the winner until the result of the photograph was called. Then it was announced: the long-time leader – the Brazilian-bred Gloria de Campeao, a 16–1 chance trained in France by Pascal Bary and ridden by T. J. Pereira – had held on by the minimum margin from 33–1 shot Lizard's Desire, owned by Sheikh Mohammed. The Godolphin representative, Allybar, was only a short head away in third, also at 16–1. Gio Ponti, 5–1, took fourth only a short head in front of Mastery, with the favourite, Gitano Hernando, sixth.

It was a well-deserved third-time-lucky for the winner, who had been runner-up to Well Armed (trained in California by Irishman Eoin Harty) the year before and eighth in 2008, and it was a race to be savoured by flat and jumping fans alike worldwide.

The splendour and wealth of Dubai are a long way from the humble, poverty-stricken world in which Tommy grew up, but his has been a rich life. With Mick retired, it was the end of more than six decades of the remarkable Kinane family in Irish racing and beyond. They have seen many tribulations, and at times they have been sorely tested, but always they were there, representing the core of the sport.

Injuries have been an inevitable part of the Kinanes' chosen way of life, but they are fighters – at times literally. It is no surprise that a good many of them have been champion boxers in their time. Perhaps more surprising is the family love of dancing. The two may seem an unlikely mix yet both require a lightness of foot. Hunting goes hand in hand with National Hunt racing, and for a number of Kinanes this has been, and is, a passion. Good old-fashioned romance has seldom been far away from the various Kinane doors.

They have done well. For one, of course, the racing life has brought global recognition and with it the role of Irish ambassador for racing worldwide. There could be no better man for that than Tommy Kinane's son, Mick.